HIDDEN KNOWLEDGE -

Unravelling the pole shift.

'The guidebook'

By Mark Elkin

This book is written in the loving memory of a true friend, a keen survivalist who followed my work avidly. He was a big part of our survival group and was one of the first members; he had his mind set on us being able to create a better world in the future without the hatred and shackles of life that is rife in today's world.

He was one of the nicest people I've ever had the pleasure of meeting. He will be sorely missed and his memories will live on forever.

Rest in peace.

Andrew Day

INTRODUCTION

In this book, we will be unravelling the mysteries of the pole shift; the connections between ancient history; ongoing geological changes of Earth; solar system influences; religious ties; CERN; HAARP; GWEN TOWERS; CHEMTRAILS; black ops; project blue beam; agenda 21; Illuminati; Disney; Masons; CIA; Elitists army; UN; New World Order; Georgia guide stones; the great pyramids; Antarctica; electromagnetism; Ether; vibration; sound; sacred geometry; numerology; symbolism; scripture; prophecy; Hopi prophecy; Nibiru; Nemesis; Orion; spirituality; survival equipment; survival locations; and many more dots that have been put together through 14 years of deep research. I will add in-depth scientific explanations to back everything up that I state.

This can be used as your pole shift guidebook. I will help explain how to survive the coming events, physically, mentally and spiritually.

Hold on to your hats, this will be a roller-coaster of a journey to the path of ultimate truth and self-discovery. You will gain a greater awareness of our 'hidden knowledge'.

CHAPTER ONE

ANCIENT CONNECTION, BIBLICAL TIES & NIBIRU.

First, we have to go back in time to understand our ancient roots. You don't have to look much further back than our ancient Sumerian ancestors to realise that a lot of our history has been masked over to cover up the true historic events that took place in those eras.

So, who are the Sumerians?

The Sumerian civilisation dates back to 4500 BC - 1900 BC, Sumer or the 'land of civilised kings'. They had the earliest settlements in the historical region of Mesopotamia which is the modern-day Iraq.

The Sumerians created an advanced civilisation with its own system of elaborate language and writing, architecture, agriculture, astronomy and mathematics.

They emerged along the flood plains of the lower reaches of the Tigris and Euphrates rivers. The bulk of the community was considered to be servant slaves of the God of the temple whilst being observed by priesthood. They are best known for inventing cuneiform script, the world's oldest extant writing system, a Latin term literally meaning 'wedged shape' – dates back to 3400 BC. It was a very sophisticated form for its day. It consisted of several hundred characters that ancient scribes used to imprint onto wet clay tablets with a reed stylus which contained syllables and words. The tablets were then left in the sun to harden or sometimes even baked.

But the real history is in the clay tablets themselves.

In 1849, British archaeologist, Austin Henry Layard discovered 22,000 of the clay tablets in the ancient city of Nineveh, the area now known as Iraq. Since then, many different cuneiform experts have been trying to translate the tablets to the best of their knowledge, some being much more accurate than others.

One of the most famous translators is author and researcher, Zecharia Sitchin, who spent over 30 years studying the mysterious clay formats. In his book 'The 12th planet', he describes an alien race called the 'Anunnaki' who came to Earth from a previously undiscovered planet in modern history called 'Nibiru'.

The tablets also depict drawings of our solar system which include Neptune, Uranus, and Pluto, amongst other planetary bodies not known to our modern day solar system that is taught in the school curriculum and it is wise to note that Uranus, initially named 'George's star', was not discovered by modern mainstream science until 1781. Neptune, at a later date in mainstream science, was discovered in 1846 and Pluto also wasn't discovered by mainstream science until 1930 which makes one wonder how the ancient Sumerians managed to map the solar system so mathematically accurate over 6000 years ago.

Not only did they depict other planetary bodies, they also gave their own accounts of how our planet was created and who were the beings responsible for our existence.

According to the tablets, the creation of Earth begins like this: --

"When in the height of heaven was not named, and the Earth beneath did not bear a name, and the primeval Aspu, who beat them, and chaos, Tiamut, the mother of them both, their waters were mingled together, and no field was formed, no marsh to be seen; when of the Gods none had been called into being, and none bore a name, and no destinies were ordained; then were created the Gods in the midst of heaven, Lahamu and Lahamu were called into being"

The tablets state that, in the beginning, there were Gods with the same resemblance as humans that ruled over Earth and all its abundance of natural elements. But there was much work to do, the Gods toiled the soil, mining for minerals to make it habitable.

It is very apparent in the translations that the Gods mutinied against their labour as it states in certain scribes: --

"When the Gods like men bore the work and suffered the toll, the toil of the Gods was great, the work was heavy, the distress was much"

It is said, because of the mutiny, 'Anu', the God of all Gods, sent his son 'Enki' or 'Ea' to ease the strain that was being caused upon the God-like men, proposed to create 'man' to bare the labour. With the help of his half-sister 'Ninki', he did just that. For this to happen, a God would have to be put to death to use the DNA of the God's blood to mix with all the natural minerals of Earths clay, with those essential materials mixed together, the first human being was created, in the likeness of Gods.

This is also apparent in the scribes: --

"You have slaughtered a God, together with his personality I have removed your heavy work, I have imposed your toil on man...in the clay, God and man shall be bound, to a unity brought together; so that to the end of days the flesh and soul which in a God have ripened- that soul in blood-kinship be bound."

Just like in the modern-day bible, the story of 'Eden' and the creation of the first 'man' are very similar to the story of the first man created in the ancient Sumerian tablets. 'Eden' is a Sumerian word for 'flat terrain' and in 12 of the tablets is a story of the 'Epic of Gilgamesh' in which Eden is mentioned as the garden of the Gods, where the DNA and clay was mixed to birth the creation of man, located in Mesopotamia between the Tigris and Euphrates rivers.

Library of Alexandria give a biblical connection to the Sumerian tablets also with some explanations from the researcher Laurence Gardner:--

According to the ancient Sumerian texts, the Sumerian God, Anu, the "supreme Lord of the Sky", the currently reigning titular head of the Sumerian Family Tree, had two sons. They were Enki (Ea), Lord of the Earth and Waters (whose mother was Antu), and Enlil (Ilu), Lord of the Air and Lord of the Command (whose mother was Ki). These two half-brothers, surprisingly, did not get along.

Critical to their rivalry, particularly from Earth's viewpoint, was the fact that Enki had been the first of the Anunnaki to hazard a trip to Earth to begin a mining operation for gold.

When this effort did not apparently produce gold in sufficient quantities, Enlil was brought in, given command, and armed with a new plan (an early version of the New Deal). The revised program was to mine gold from deep mines in the Earth.

According to Sumerian texts (as detailed in Genesis of the Grail Kings [1]), during a visit by their father, Anu (the archetypal absentee landlord), the Anunnaki made a decision:--

> *"The Gods had clasped their hands together, Had cast lots and had divided. Anu then went up to heaven. To Enlil the Earth was made subject. The seas, enclosed as with a loop, They had given to Enki, the Prince of Earth."*

Sounds fair. However, as Laurence Gardner points out, "Enki was not happy about his brother's promotion because, although Enlil was the elder of the two, his mother (Ki) was Anu's junior sister, whereas Enki's mother (Antu) was the senior sister. True kingship, claimed Enki, progressed as a matrilineal institution through the female line, and by this right of descent Enki maintained that he was the first born of the royal succession."

*"I am the great brother of the Gods.
I am he who has been born as the first son of
the divine Anu."*

If there is a philosophy of Enki, it manifests and explains itself in early Mesopotamian and Egyptian thought, where the true creator of the universe was manifest within nature, and that nature enveloped both the Anunnaki, and the humans. Nature, as the Great Mother, was still supreme, despite any patriarchal scheme to the contrary. Admittedly, Enki's claim of his birth right, the one being based on a matrilineal succession, essentially the mitochondria DNA link, which is wholly passed through the female line, was in Enki's best interests. But Enki was also the maternal grandfather who came to the aid of Inanna when things went badly during her Descent into the Underworld.

With the arrival of Enlil, however, who in his best interests must demean the matriarchal line of succession, and thus nature itself, everything changed. The Great Mother was dethroned and replaced by a supreme male (as opposed to a male consort for the Queen). The idea of cooperation, as exemplified by the council of Anunnaki making cooperative decisions, was quickly replaced by competition, and harmony was forsaken in favour of subservience. The supreme God became abstract, and any physical connection with human or nature was lost -- and thus the link between nature and human also destroyed. When Enlil hit town, there was a whole new deal put into effect.

According to Laurence Gardner [1], "The dominant tenet of the new thought was based wholly on the utmost fear of Enlil, who was known to have instigated the great Flood [or else acquiesced in not warning the humans, or making any attempt to save them], and to have facilitated the invasion and destruction of civilized Sumer. Here was a deity who spared no mercy for those who did not comply with his dictatorial authority.

"Abraham had experienced the vengeful Enlil first hand at the fall of Ur, and he was not about to take any chances with his own survival. He was even prepared to sacrifice the life of his young son, Isaac, to appease the implacable God (Genesis 32:-9)." The oriental scholar Henri Frankfort summarized the situation by making the point that... 'Those who served Jehovah must forego the richness, the fulfilment, and the consolation of a life which moves in tune with the great rhythms of the Earth and sky."

Bramley [3] has noted that, "We therefore find Ea [Enki] as the reputed culprit who tried to teach early man (Adam) the way to spiritual freedom. This suggests that Ea intended his creation, Homo sapiens, to be suited for Earth labour, but at some point, he changed his mind about using spiritual enslavement as a means."

From a Biblical perspective, it was Enki who (with the critical assistance of his half-sister, Ninki, aka Nin-khursag) created Adam and Eve. It was Enlil, on the other hand, who created "Edin". Enki was the serpent in the garden, who urged Adam and Eve to eat of the fruit of the Tree of Knowledge of Good and Evil (which was infinitely beneficial to their spiritual growth). It was Enlil, who drove them out of Edin, while Enki was there to clothe them. It is worth noting that Zecharia Sitchin [2] claims that the biblical word for "snake" is nahash, which comes from the root word NHSH, and which means "to decipher, to find out." In other words, Enki, the God of Wisdom.

In the time of Noah, it was Enlil who either created the Great Deluge/Flood as a means of wiping out mankind (because they supposedly made too much noise), or else refused to warn the humans or do anything to save them or help them to save themselves. Enki, on the other hand, apparently against orders of the Anunnaki (who Enlil now controlled), provided the boat plans for Noah to build his Ark, and thus save him, his family (and likely a fair number of helpful artisans and their families). Enki included as well the seed of other living things (a "natural" kind of thing to do).

In the Sumerian texts, we have the stories of Enki and Enlil, and for the most part there is portions devoted to each. But in Genesis, Enlil seemingly reigns supreme. Enlil knew early on that a pound of good Public Relations effort is worth a ton of truth.

Abraham and his descendants served Enlil and followed his precepts. The Egyptians, on the other hand, were Enki's protégés, and based on food management practices during the devastating droughts around the time of Jacob and Joseph, were doing a lot better than Enlil's followers. Obviously, Noah backed the right horse in that Enki shared boat plans with the righteous fellow, whom Enlil later claimed as his own.

But at one point, circa 2000 B.C.E., all hell broke loose. In an all-out war of Enki's humans against Enlil's humans, complete with all manner of diplomatic subterfuge in the mix, Sodom and Gomorrah took the brunt of the action and were destroyed by nuclear weaponry. They were A-bombed. The decision for this, however, was not, as you might have expected, due to Enlil's instigation. Instead, it was due to the actions of his sons, Ninurta and Nangal. The (radioactive) fallout of their actions then resulted in the final destruction of the Sumerian civilisation (circa 2000 B.C.E.). Curiously, this event in the Annals of Earth turned out to be something of a Waterloo for Enlil. Not that the guy (dba "God") fled the scene, but thereafter, the idea of unilateral actions was a bit more constrained. Enlil was no longer the undisputed Lord of the Command among his peers.

Which might be just as well. As Laurence Gardner [1] phrased it:-- "This muddled and unparalleled concept of Jehovah being right when he was wrong, honest when he was dishonest, was born out of an inherent fear of his vengeful power and unbounded wrath. Whether as Jehovah (in Genesis) or as Enlil (in Mesopotamian record) it was he who had instigated the Semitic invasions which led to the 'confusion of tongues' and the fall of Sumer. It was he who had brought about the devastating Flood, and it was he who had levelled the cities of Sodom and Gomorrah, not because of their wickedness, as related in Genesis (18-19), but because of the wisdom and insight of their inhabitants, as depicted in the Coptic Paraphrase of Shem. It was Jehovah who had removed the Israelites from their homeland and sending them into seventy years of captivity by King Nebuchadnezzar II and his five Babylonian successors down to King Belshazzer (545-539 BC)."

This latter event is critical as another turning point in the Enki and Enlil warfare, as it reflects a time, circa 600 B.C.E., when Enlil was stepping back from the overt control of Earth. (A fact which does not necessarily imply stepping back from covert control!)

Zecharia Sitchin [2] has taken a different, decidedly pro-Jehovah, pro-Enlil approach in his writings. While admitting to the complicity of Enlil's sons in the destruction of Sodom and Gomorrah, Sitchin tends to blame the female (i.e. Inanna) for seducing King Shulgi of Ur (and thus destroying a once thriving civilisation). Sitchin also charges Enki's son, Marduk, who became the Babylonian God, with being perhaps the prime culprit of all the bad news that was extant in what Sitchin refers to as "The Fateful Century" (2123 - 2023). At one point in his book, The Wars of God and Men, Sitchin writes: -- "There was great jubilation in the land when the great temple was rededicated to Enlil and Ninlil [Enlil's wife], in the year 1953 B.C.E.; it was only then that the cities of Sumer and Akkad were officially declared habitable again."

And just guess who was responsible for them being uninhabitable in the first place?

To appreciate the continuing sage of Enki versus Enlil, it is instructive to note their place in the Sumerian Family Tree, aka the "Grand Assembly of the Anunnaki".

Marduk (who would become the God of the Babylonians) was Enki's first born, and that of Enki's wife, the Goddess Damkina. Enki's other wife was his half-sister, Nin-khursag (meaning "Mountain Queen"), the Lady of Life, also known as Nin-mah, the Great Lady.

Enlil was also espoused to Nin-khursag and their son was Ninurta (Ningirsu), the Mighty Hunter. By another wife, Ninlil (Sud), Enlil had a second son, Nanna (Suen), known as the Bright One. Nanna and his wife, Ningal, were the parents of Inanna (who was called Ishtar by the Babylonians), and who married the Shepherd King Dumu-zi (the latter given in the Semitic Old Testament book of Ezekiel 8:14 as Tammuz).

Another son of Enlil and Ninlil was Nergal (Meslamtaea), King of the Underworld. He married Eresh-kigal, the Queen of the Netherworld, the daughter of Nanna and Ningal (i.e. Inanna's sister), and the mother of Lilith (who became handmaiden to Inanna, her maternal aunt). Lilith is also notorious as the first wife of Adam, but it was Lilith who rejected him (and thus incurred the wrath of every reject-worthy male on the planet).

By some accounts, Inanna was also the granddaughter of Enki (as well as Enlil). This strange situation was critical in Inanna's classic tale of her Descent into the Underworld. (I.e. Enlil turned a blind eye, while Enki saved Inanna's lovely little family.) Even more crucial to the plot was the fact that Inanna was also a favourite of the supreme Anu. Thus, she was never, never at a loss as to what she thought she could do and get away with. Her story has been well told two books by Susan Ferguson:- Inanna Returns and Inanna, Hyper luminal. (Ms. Ferguson does include Enki's son, Marduk, as the bad guy, but on the other hand, keeps Enki as a favourite. She can do that. It's her books.)

Speaking of Marduk, not only was he the arch-enemy of Inanna (thus explaining Susan's plotting), but Marduk thoroughly angered just about everyone about him. Even his father, Enki, must have wondered where he went wrong in raising his first son, a question not uncommon to any father. At the same time, it must be admitted, Marduk was without question a serious pain in the rear (and elsewhere) for Enlil, and thus Enki might have had moments of genuine pride.

Just as Enki may have been given temporary, overt control over the Earth during the Age of Pisces, Marduk, who was identified with the planet Mars, and thus the astrological sign of Aries, had assumed he would be in charge during the Age of Aries. Depending on the time allotted to each sign, whether it is 1/12th, or more likely the actual time spent in the sign, Marduk's Age of Aries likely ran from roughly

2,000 B.C.E. to about 600 B.C.E. This was his time, therefore, and The Wars of Gods and Men told by Sitchin was in large part Marduk's attempts to wrest control from Enlil, and the Anunnaki who supported the latter. The fact that it became a very messy war was not necessarily Marduk's fault.

For the fact remains that, circa 1950 B.C.E., after Enlil's son, Ninurta, had failed to rally the Anunnaki troops on his own behalf and thoroughly bombed on his venture to Sodom and Gomorra, Marduk finally got his chance.

"Lord Anu, lord of the Gods who from Heaven came to Earth, and Enlil, lord of Heaven and Earth who determines the destinies of the land, Determined for Marduk, the firstborn of Enki, the Enlil-functions over all mankind; Made him great among the Gods who watch and see, Called Babylon by name to be exalted, made it supreme in the world; And established for Marduk, in its midst, an everlasting kingship."

Marduk, from Babylon, ultimately took vengeance on the Enlil supporters known as the Hebrews, who had opposed Marduk's reign, and they thereafter spent seventy years in captivity. During this time, Enlil never raised a hand to assist them. In Enlil's view, they were quite expendable. Obviously, someone, unlike their ancestral patriarch, Noah, had failed to back the right horse.

For some time (i.e. the Age of Aries), Marduk took over Enlil's subjugation of the humans, politics of the slavery kind made strange bedfellows. But the Age of Aries (unlike the Age of Pisces) was mercifully short. And it had the decided advantage of prepping the Anunnaki for Enki's take over about 600 B.C.E., when the Age of Pisces began.

Many translations of the clay tablets also state that human beings were unable to reproduce on their own which lead to the later manipulation of our DNA by Enki and Ninki. Because of the help of the two Godly figures, the first fully functional and independent human being was created called 'Adapa'.

However, Enki did not seek the approval from his brother Enlil before creating humans that could reproduce. This enraged Enlil, a conflict between the Gods continued because Enlil saw humans as slaves, whereas Enki wanted humans to develop into our own civilisation without being bound by the chains of labour.

There can be many comparisons made when you study the Sumerian tablets and the bible, many similar stories just spoken in different ways.

It is also important to point out that many researchers in these studies seem to agree that gold was of the upmost importance to mine for, according to the ancient code, on Earth, gold is one of the most important resources society knows of. We use it in a lot of things. It is used in electrical components and in almost everything that has to do with electricity, gold is really one of the top conductors, and its malleability and ability to transform it into wires, the ability to use it in really small forms as nanoparticles is going to make it an incredible technological resource for any sort of intelligent life form, so you would believe that an alien race with the ability to travel through space uses gold in more than one form. Gold can also be used as an energy source through properties called thermoelectric effects, where it can take heat and turn it directly into electricity, this means obtaining clean and efficient energy.

Gold reflects infrared light. Infrared is basically light you don't see it, but in fact, interact with it in the form of heat, the radiation interacts with our molecules and that makes them vibrate faster and you'll feel that as heat, gold also makes a good heat shield, partly because it's quite malleable. Better yet you can make gold very thin; it's easy to work with; and it has great properties for reflecting and heat protection making it truly the only metal that is proven to last the test of time- we can say that Gold is indestructible. Ancient civilisations used it thousands of years ago in figures and some of them in buildings, anything that was made out of gold- thousands of years ago still exists today. Not only in ancient Sumeria, but ancient civilisation across the globe had a very special place for gold in their society.

 As Sitchin theorised that "the Anunnaki" came from another planet in our solar system that has a 3,600-year elliptical orbit. The planets minerals and resources were depleting, specifically Gold. The Annika's home planet needed gold in the atmosphere which was disappearing so they basically came to Earth to mine gold and take it back to their home planet.

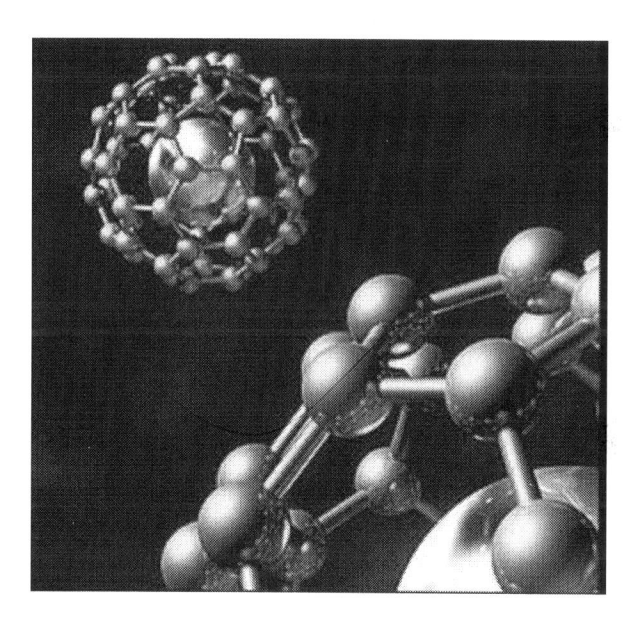

According to the Ancient Alien theory, the Anunnaki genetically altered primitive mankind for the exact reason to create a labour force, which allowed them to mine gold faster.

Nibiru is part of a mini solar system that that is called the 'Nemesis system', nemesis is a brown dwarf star which has 7 orbiting planets.

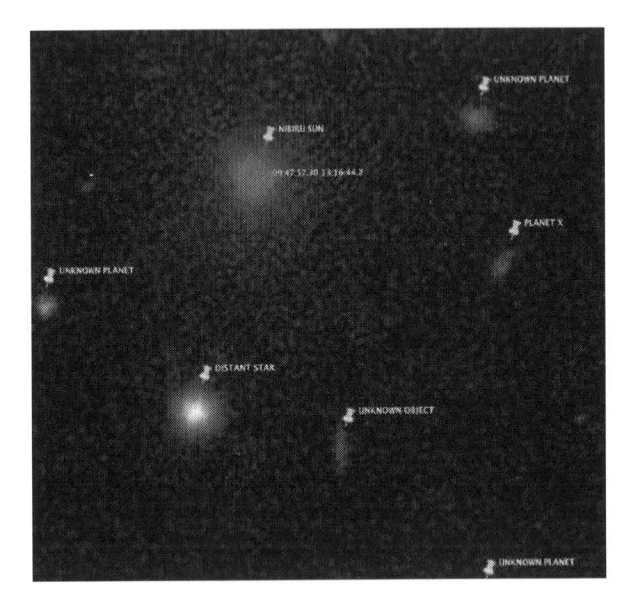

Nibiru is also referred to in ancient text as the 'planet of crossing' and many studies have depicted the planet as the 'winged planet', which is the outer most orbiting planet of nemesis and is the culprit that causes the pole shift, nemesis is the main body that causes all the geological changes of Earth as it draws closer to Earths orbital path every year due to its very dense electromagnetic particle makeup.

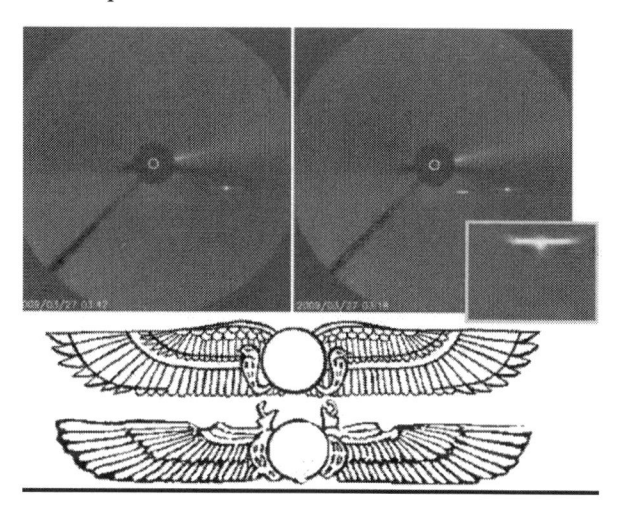

It's all related to the crossing, every scripture, every religion, everything that has been happening in the past millennials, wars, battles, famine, the Earthquake increase, the volcanic increase, the lightning storms, the wild fires, the suns behaviour, the fireball increase, the flooding, the fish dying, the land animals dying.

There are 7 orbiting planets that's orbit nemesis. (7 angels/7 trumpets etc) it's all how it's interpreted but I can assure you it all points to the crossing in the 'end days' that brings the 'tribulation' on Earth, .it will take 7 years for Earth to go back to normal after the pole shift and it's a '7-year tribulation', coincidence? I'll let you be the judge.

The last survivors of the pole shift handed down these coded prophecies or spoke through the word of God- your choice which one you believe, I do not judge.

It's all written to tell us what's coming, it's here.
BLOOD=red iron oxide particles.
ANGELS= planetary bodies
DAY NOT SHINE=perihelion (sun goes dark)
JUDGING BY THESE PROPHECIES THE INTERPRETATIONS CAN BE TAKEN AS YOU WILL- I am in no way saying they are categorically correct, just different interpretations that all have the same connections.

"Because of this the land dries up, and all who live in it waste away; the beasts of the field, the birds in the sky and the fish in the sea are swept away."
Hosea 4:3

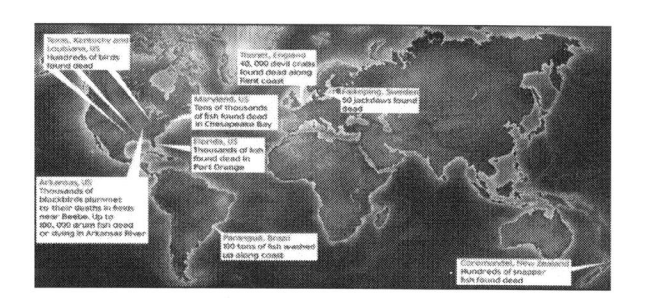

Dead walruses found on Alaska beach

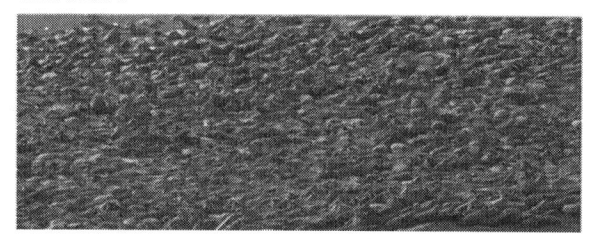

*"Immediately after the distress of those days"
'the sun will be darkened, and the moon will*

not give its light; the stars will fall from the sky, and the heavenly bodies will be shaken.'
Matthew 24:29-31:29

"And I saw, when he had opened the sixth seal: - and behold there was a great Earthquake. And the sun became black as sackcloth of hair: - and the whole moon became as blood. And the stars from heaven fell upon the Earth, as the fig tree casteth its green figs when it is shaken by a great wind. And the heaven departed as a book folded up. And every mountain, and the islands, were moved out of their places. And the kings of the Earth and the princes and tribunes and the rich and the strong and every bondman and every freeman hid themselves in the dens and in the rocks of mountains..."
Following the opening of the Sixth Seal "...there was silence in heaven, as it were for half an hour..." [Apocalypse 8:1];

"afterwards, seven angels are given seven trumpets:-"...And the angel took the censer and filled it with the fire of the altar and cast it on the Earth:- and there were thunders and voices and lightnings and a great Earthquake." And the seven angels who had the seven trumpets prepared themselves to sound the trumpets..."And the first angel sounded the

trumpet:- and there followed hail and fire, mingled with blood:- and it was cast on the Earth. And the third part of the Earth was burnt up:- and the third part of the trees was burnt up:- and all green grass was burnt up."
"And the second angel sounded the trumpet:- and, as it were, a great mountain, burning with fire, was cast into the sea. And the third part of the sea became blood...And the third part of those creatures died which had life in the sea:- and the third part of the ships was destroyed."
"And the third angel sounded the trumpet:- and a great star fell from heaven, burning as it were a torch. And it fell on the third part of the rivers and upon the fountains of waters:- And the name of the star is called Wormwood. And the third part of the waters became wormwood. And many men died of the waters, because they were made bitter."
"And the fourth angel sounded the trumpet:- and the third part of the sun was smitten, and the third part of the moon, and the third part of the stars, so that the third part of them was darkened. And the day did not shine for a third part of it:- and the night in like manner. And I beheld:- and heard the voice of one eagle flying through the midst of heaven, saying with a loud voice:- Woe, Woe, Woe to the inhabitants of the Earth, by reason of the

rest of the voices of the three angels, who are yet to sound the trumpet!"

"And the fifth angel sounded the trumpet:- and I saw a star fall from heaven upon the Earth. And there was given to him the key of the bottomless pit. And he opened the bottomless pit:- and the smoke of the pit arose, as the smoke of a great furnace. And the sun and the air were darkened with the smoke of the pit. And from the smoke of the pit there came out locusts upon the Earth. And power was given to them, as the scorpions of the Earth have power. And it was commanded them that they should not hurt the grass of the Earth nor any green thing nor any tree:- but only the men who have not the sign of God on their foreheads. And it was given unto them that they should not kill them:- but that they should torment them five months. And their torment was as the torment of a scorpion when he striketh a man. And in those days, men shall seek death and shall not find it. And they shall desire to die:- and death shall fly from then. And the shapes of the locusts were like unto horses prepared unto battle. And on their heads were, as it were, crowns like gold:- and their faces were as the faces of men. And they had hair as the hair of women:- and their teeth were as lions. And they had breastplates as breastplates of iron:- and the noise of their *wings was as the noise of chariots and many horses running to battle. And they had tails like to scorpions:- and there were stings in their tails. And their power was to hurt men, five months. And they had over them A king, the angel of the bottomless pit (whose name in Hebrew is Abaddon and in Greek Apollyon, in Latin Exterminans)."*

The tale of the Opening of the Seven Seals describes a series of events that occurred or that are still ongoing (the first five Seals) or that still have to come (Sixth and Seventh Seal) shortly.

About the last two seals, their opening will cause plenty of catastrophes and destructions, marked by the sound of "seven trumpets":-- the darkening of the Sun, of the Moon and the Stars; precipitation and collisions; yet it is remarkable the mention of a "...star fall from heaven upon the Earth. And there was given to him the key of the bottomless pit". An eerie comparison could be made with the coming of Nibiru? The planet that, according to all my research/ancient depictions/wall carvings/paintings and the studies above, would bring along darkness and electromagnetic troubles on Earth.

It is hard to interpret the "coming of the Locusts" out from the smoke; the similarity with the Locusts' invasion of the Ancient Egypt it is scarcely probable, for this part of the Apocalypse is supposed to reveal future events; something more logic, yet shocking, would be assuming that Nibiru is a dwelled planet (Sumerians believed so and heavily depicted this in their carvings/writings) in this case the biblical excerpt meaningful and truthful.

"In the firmament of the sky all the stars will be in the daylight shown, together with the two luminaries, in the rapid and sudden fall of time...A darkening, thick night shall cover the infinite disc of Earth...Then a mighty stream of blazing flame will flow from the sky and will annihilate the royal creation...The Moon and the shining Sun shall merge into one, and everywhere is desert and desolation...From the sky stars will fall upon the ocean...and the whole air will be shaken, and filled with angels, that will fight among themselves the whole day"-

The paragraph speaks upon the slowing of the terrestrial Motus, while the fall of the star could be the consequence of the sudden change of the Earth axis' angle, so giving the illusion that the stars would actually fall into the sea or its referring to the meteorites it will bring with the tail of Nibiru that will rain down on Earth.

The Apocalypses of Ephesus Prophecy would have been dictated to a XIV century hermit by ab angel from the Church of Ephesus. The following passage speaks upon the arrival of a new celestial body: --

"...Over the mountains of blood...shall fall the stars, whilst the Sun shall swallow the Moon and then two new lights will throw up...Earth's wounds shall still bleeding...but the flood will no longer be of water, but of fire...All shall turn into a sea of blood...It will be on these days of universal madness that the Antichrist will come...from the East, bearing signs of righteousness and wellness...Many shall follow Death, confusing it with the Lamb of Peace...and Many shall desert, when terror...will fall upon Rome...Whilst the sky will show the signs of the Great Day, that are the Cross [Christianity], the half-moon [Islamism], and the beheaded eagle [the Antichrist]...In the marked time the Sun will be ordered to cry. And the tears of the Sun shall fall upon Earth...Huge Sparkles shall then spring up from different places on Earth.

And each Sparkle shall turn into a plague. And each plague shall bleed salty water and bones' dust...Rome, in this time, shall change its name...and the legion of the Antichrist will march through Rome. And the ground of Rome shall move as the wave of the sea. And the sea will come to Rome...The seed of life shall stand in the Glen of the Four Saints. From there the history shall start again...Within the new garden...new laws...time shall have...dimensions, And the Sun shall give a different warmth."-

Here we read about a derangement of our Solar System, which would cause massive damages near Earth to an extent that the Moon would collapse. The "days of universal madness" could refer to the misbalance of the planets, while the "crying Sun" could link to an intense, radioactive solar-rain, that will lead to the overheating of the atmosphere and would increase dryness on Earth

"...the ground of Rome shall move as the wave of the sea...", this could refer to a violent quake that would be produced and that could even sink the Eternal City ("...And the sea will come to Rome...").

The outcome of all this chain of catastrophes predicted by the Apocalypse of Ephesus would be that of a complete reshaping of our planet, which perhaps will spin through a different orbit. The line *"...And the Sun shall give a different warmth"*, could even refer to a new Solar System but really means Earth being in a new position due to the pole shift.
Michel de Notre Dame (1503-1566), also known as Nostradamus, was physician, philosopher, scientist and astrologist. He predicted several occurrences from 1555 to 3797, among them, he spoke about the coming of the Antichrist, that will cause years of terror and blood before the new Golden Age begins. This age would allegedly re-establish the correct balance on Earth.
The Century X, quatrain 72, says: -- "L'an mil neuf cens nonante neuf sept mois viendra un grand Roy d'effrayeur:- , (In the year 1999, seventh month, du ciel:- From the sky will come a great King of Terror.

Resusciter le grand Roy d'Angolmois, to bring back to life the great king of Angolmois, Auant apres Mars regner par bon-heur." Before and after Mars is to reign by good luck)." The date clearly refers to the Solar Eclipses occurred on August 199 (the difference of one month is due to the change of the Gregorian Calendar made in 1582); according to Nostradamus, that year saw the coming of the Antichrist whose kingdom will last 27 years, before the beginning of the Golden Age.

The objective difficulty upon the interpretation of Nostradamus' prophecies (and of prophecies in general) is a fact, however, we can attempt to give it a possible interpretation, that is on August 1999 a big planet will come "from the sky" that will wreak havoc on Earth and will dominate Space "before and after Mars" (our Solar System?).

Even though no descent of the "King of Terror" occurred in 1999, it's to be outlined how on the same year a "Planet X" was actually discovered and that it's been causing progressive Earth changes for the past 20 years when it entered our solar system, coincidence?

To the Century II, quatrain 41, Nostradamus writes:-- La grand' estoille par sept iours bruslera, (The great star will burn for seven days, Nuee fera deux soleils apparoir:-- The cloud will cause two suns to appear:-- Le gros mastin toute nuit hurlera, the big mastiff will howl all night.

Quand grand pontife changera de terroir.
When the great pontiff will change country)
The hint to a "second sun" is quiet interesting especially if linked to the second half of the quatrain, that that connect the "mastiff" to the end of Christianity.

Who, or what, is the mastiff? What does the Howling mean? A signal, the changing sign of our religious concept following the arrival of the "second sun" (the quatrain doesn't speak of a shining "second sun" but it describes its appearance because of the blazing of a "great star" therefore we cannot deny the hypothesis of the second sun being the black sun mentioned by other prophecies).

Century I, quatrain 69, contains the description of a round mount that will cause the sinking of big countries (maybe continents).

Saint John, on his Apocalypse, speaks of "*a great mountain, burning with fire, was cast into the sea.*" [Apocalypses 8:-8], although the latter refers to an object coming from outer space.
" La grande montagne ronde de sept stades (The great mountain, 4,247 feet in circumference, Apres paix, guerre, faim, inondation, After peace, war, famine, flooding,

Roulera loin abimant grands contrades Will spread far, drowning great countries Memes antiques, et grande fondation." Even antiquities and their mighty foundations.)

Giordano Bruno (1548-1600), left some notes upon the future of the Mankind:--

"Man shall travel the cosmos and from cosmos he shall learn about the day of the ending...Just when the man will believe to be the lord of the Universe, many wealthy cities will end like Sodom and Gomorrah...A black sun will swallow in the space the sun, the moon, and all the planets orbiting around the sun..."-

Here the black sun is clearly mentioned. It could refer to a planet bearing so great a mass to be compared to the sun. The black sun could even refer to the "twin" of the sun, Nemesis (whose existence has been suggested recently), name created by Richard A. Muller to this celestial body. Nemesis would be a red/brown dwarf whose discovery has yet to come. As such, Nemesis could not generate light.(infrared spectrum) Following the theory of our Solar system as a binary system, the prophecy could describe Nemesis "swallowing" the sun.

The Black Spider, a German monk who lived in the XVI Century, provides a list of occurrences on his yearly prophecies. The year 2000, that he calls "Glory of the Fire", represents a crucial turn for the history of mankind, a starting point towards a new spiritual path, which will mark radical, physical changes:--

"*When the mankind will reach the end of the Millennium, it will have climbed over the hilltop and from up above it shall see the wreckage of a time and the path which leads to the new Earthly Heaven. The first generation walking on that path will be a generation in pain, for hard shall be the path to regain the joy of the spirit*"

According to the monk, the mankind shall have to walk "under the bridge of the five pains" before reaching the "joys of the spirit". The prophecy speaks of fifty years of plagues, who are deemed necessary to the conquest of the "Earthly Heaven". Between 2000 and 2010 there will be "the time of fears"; followed by "the decade of madness", "the decade of settlement", and "the decade of resumption".

The Black Spider claims that:- "Christ dies along the Tiber and arises on the Volga" It seems the Christianity is doomed to be wiped out of the Mediterranean - where it rose - to come back further North.

The Black Spider speaks upon the "Black Prince", the Antichrist as:-

"There will be a new voice that the temple will demolish...Here he comes! [the Antichrist] descends from the sunny road standing on a carriage dragged by four black horses. He bears the colour of the snow, His voice bears the force of thunder . Firm is his hand, a command is his gesture. There, among the stones of the last amphitheatre the blood flows. The tablets of the law shall throw in the dust and stamped on by the horses' iron. Men! Pitiful, crawling creatures, the Prince gives you his law:- rejoice until drunkenness and you will be happy; Worship Caesar and you will be

exalted; steal, and you will be honoured...The Black Prince shall hold a banquet in the hall of the Great Dome and thousands of fishermen shall incense his hand:- a hand which holds the power of life and death, a hand which destroy and create, a hand which bless and annihilate...Cry, mothers! Throw your bowels in the fire. Tear your womb apart...Man shall no longer be born from woman, for He came, the last son of Osiris. So it was written...yet do not cry...It's time for eyes to shut. Because the vine shall no longer give wine. And the Earth shall no longer produce wheat. So it will be, until the new day we shall seek in the infinite...This will be the chant of the six legions crossing the river. Beware to the swamp, Here shall fall the last hope of the little Caesar. There will be signs from the sky. There will be the voices of the dead, There will be the moans of the living".

The Black Spider reminds of how "signs from the sky" and "other phenomena" will trouble the peaceful. The monk's prophecies end with the passage:-

"Humanity has been marked by three floods:- the first was made of water, the second will be of fire, the third shall be made of stars...at the third flood" [2500-3000 AD circa] "the sky

shall go off forever" [The Apocalypse of Ephesus speaks identically upon the Flood of Fire]The Monk Basil (1660-1722), a russian prophet from the orthodox Convent of Kalnin, experienced, during his life several "aesthatic visions" concerning the future of the mankind; Basil wrote all of his visions in prose, like the following:-"Upon the golden lamb the stars shall fall, and it will become ash. An empire shall fall and a pyramid will be shaken by the erathquake, for a blasphemous use was made od the Eternal. Gold will turn into ash and ash into gold:- the country on whose rivers flows honey, shall become the country of starvation, where Cain and Abel shall dwell. Nothing shall last of the stars. On the time when the golden lamb will be destroyed (that will be the time of the marine beast) you shall see signs in the sky and on Earth. The Sun will change its path and the moon will be lost among the mountains, the stars shall fall upon Earth and from East a voice shall raise, which will be heard till the West. Invisible mountains shall go through the sky, and when one of them shall be seen, there will be no more time to pray. You shall then hear the cries of thousand mothers, for thousand men shall be crushed by the mountain. Within the time of the marine beast the sky will cast its messages so that no man will come unprepared to the final day. Legions of Saints will come through the clouds, when Earth will be besieged by Satan. The angels will speak to the men, albeit few could hear their voice and few could see the angelic visions. Millions of heavenly spirits shall dwell the sky and millions of demons shall dwell the Earth:- the former, dressed with light, the latter, of selfishness and wickedness. On the day of the three Saints, the shining spirits will descend on Earth to carry the crown of righteousness, and a despairing cry shall be heard in the valley of the golden lamb".

The passage "...The Sun will change its path...there will be no more time to pray..." could refer to the appearance of a new planet in the Solar System, planet which would produce changes on our planet such as the axis tilting ..This would lead to place the Earth on different coordinates to the Sun and constellations. Furthermore "The day will come on which you shall find the Black Sea over the Urals and the Caspian Sea upon the Volga highlands, for everything shall change...where there was once ice, now it shall burn the Sun...citrus...shall be collected from the ground of...Russia, whilst ice will rule over Northern Africa..."..As well as in the Black Spider's prophecies ("Christ dies along the

Tiber and arises on the Volga"), here too is Russia the land of the "change"; deep and radical changes are expected, caused by the arrival of something "from the sky", from outer space, that is.

It is not certain in these prophecies whether it will be a meteor, a planet or any other celestial body however its impact against our planet will cause dramatic electromagnetic and climate changes. [the "change" coming from the East is the same prophecy mentioned by Apocalypse of Ephesus and by the Black Spider].

On January 7, 1950, Mother Elena Aiello had a vision:-

"...When an extraordinary sign will appear in the sky, men shall know the punishment of the world is near!..."

What could be such an extraordinary sign? The Hale-Bopp comet, passed by the Earth in 1997 and visible only every 4200 years, could provide the answer?

Among the effects the arrival of Nibiru could cause on Earth - reversal of the Poles and axis tilting a deceleration of the planet Motus is feared. Such deceleration would lead to a complete, three-day stop of the Earth's rotation, as the "Prophecies of the Three Days of Darkness" state:-

"...Great Darkness will come upon Earth and shall last three days and three nights... On those three days artificial light will be impossible...all (the enemies of the church) shall perish on Earth during this universal darkness except...those few who shall convert to elect a new Pope..." - [Blessed Anna Maria Taigi (1837)
]
"...On the three days of Darkness...only a fourth of the mankind shall last..." Nun Maria Gesù Crocifisso di Pau (1878)]

"...The one who will last to the Three Days of Darkness...shall seem to himself as the only one...for...the workd shall be covered with corpses..." [S. Gaspare del Bufalo (1837)]

On April 7, 1913, Padre Pio da Pietralcina spoke upon the Three Days of Darkness and pointed at May as the month of the change:-

"Hurricanes of fire will be thrown from the clouds, and will spread all over the Earth. Storms, Tempests, endless thunders and raining, Earthquakes shall be all over the Earth

during the Three Days. A restless rain of fire will follow, to show that God is the Lord of Creation....On the third night Earthquakes and fire will cease, and the next day the sun will shine again. Angels will descend from the sky, carrying the spirit of peace upon Earth. One third of the mankind shall perish...Be prepared to live three days of a complete darkness. These three days are very close...and during these days you will be as dead, without eating nor drinking. Then, the light will return. Yet many will be those who won't see it again...Many people will run in terror. They will run with no destination. They will say salvation is to the East and people will run eastward, but will fall down a precipice..They will say salvation is to the West, and people will run westward, but will fall in a furnace...The Earth will shake and great will be the panic...the Earth is sick. Earthquake will be like the serpent:- you shall hear it crawling everywhere. Many stones will fall. And many people will die..A meteor shall fall upon Earth and all will thrill. It will be a catastrophe, by far worse than a war. many things will be erased. And this will be one of the signs...

...You will go through dramatic moments...Beware to the month of May. I still see floods and Earthquakes...I see blood. Poor

Italy...it is going towards bad violence...Pray for the Three Days which you shall live...take some provisions...for at least three months..."

Jelaila Starr, an American sensorial who claims to be in contact with Nibiru, receives telepathic messages on regular basis from the stars. She describes Nibiru as a planet dwelled by many races, a planet that can move along and outside its orbit, as a real spacecraft. The following passage - one among several messages received by the Nibiruans - indicates the consequences of the arrival of Nibiru to our planet:-

"Nibiru stands as the primary stimulator for our spiritual rebirthing. When it will be sufficiently close to Earth...it will show...the ancient knoledge, suppressed by the religions and by the governs so to control people, will rise...The effects of its great magnetic field..are already affecting us...Nibiru is affecting the Sun...increasing the solar wind...the solar emissions..[The Sun] is emitting more light..."

Jelaila says that Nibiru would already be somewhere within our Solar System, even though she doesn't give any precise indication upon when it is supposed to show up. Despite the appealing content of the messages, there is more than one doubt regarding the scientific substance of Jelaila's revelations. Moreover these messages convey quite a different meaning than the aforementioned prophecies, which bring together the vision of a "cosmic catastrophism". But who knows? All a coincidence? I don't think so.

Another sensorial who claims to be in contact with an alien race - a reptilian race - from Nibiru is Nancy Lieder (Zeta talk) according to her, the Mankind would be close to a big turn following the entrance of Nibiru into our Solar System.

Nancy is carrying out this message since 1995, along with a campaign of information aimed to make people aware upon an approaching, global catastrophe that will occur when an enormous planet will come nearby the Earth. This planet, Nibiru, would have been known by ancient civilisations and yet to be discovered by the modern scientists. However, she explains a pole shift that concurs with the 'three days of darkness' and links to all other prophecies.the more you research, the more you realise that zetatalk is a CIA deep black OP run programme and Nancy lieder is a CIA operative that only ever gives half truths mixed with tons of disinformation. They have made predictions that have been very wrong but also made some that have been right, especially in the last 3 years , I would always advise to take everything they say with a pinch of salt.

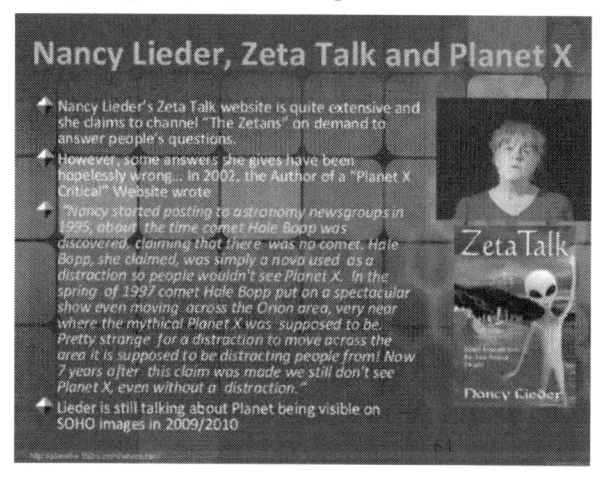

Nancy Lieder, Zeta Talk and Planet X

- Nancy Lieder's Zeta Talk website is quite extensive and she claims to channel "The Zetans" on demand to answer people's questions.
- However, some answers she gives have been hopelessly wrong... in 2002, the Author of a "Planet X Critical" Website wrote
  "Nancy started posting to astronomy newsgroups in 1995, about the time comet Hale Bopp was discovered, claiming that there was no comet. Hale Bopp, she claimed, was simply a nova used as a distraction so people wouldn't see Planet X. In the spring of 1997 comet Hale Bopp put on a spectacular show even moving across the Orion area, very near where the mythical Planet X was supposed to be. Pretty strange for a distraction to move across the area it is supposed to be distracting people from! Now 7 years after this claim was made we still don't see Planet X, even without a distraction."
- Lieder is still talking about Planet being visible on SOHO images in 2009/2010

V.M.Rabolù, 'true master whose special powers allowed him to search upon the most enigmatic events of our time', wrote a book on the last years of his life.

"Hercolubus, or the Red Planet", is about the upcoming of a gigantic planet into our Solar System. This planet, bigger than Jupiter, would have a wide orbit which leads it outside the Solar System during is cycle, its return, every thousands of years, would cause deep disasters and changes. It seems that its last passage occurred during the Atlantis Era, whose end could have been the consequence of geological catastrophes and electromagnetic unbalances.

Hercolubus' arrival would have already produced certain phenomena on Earth, such as the increasing of Earthquakes, tsunami, hurricanes (700% more since 1971). Rabolù speaks about pollution of the seas and the atmosphere, about nuclear experiments that caused mutations and deformations in many countries.

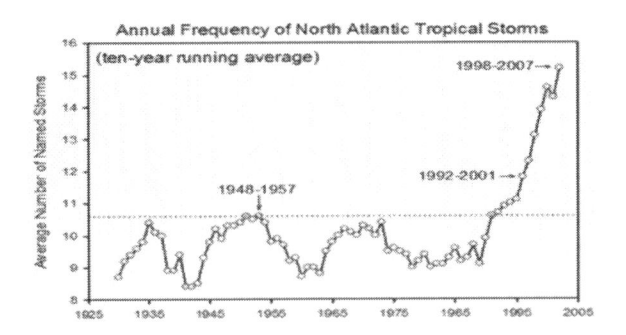

"What I hereby state is a prophecy that will soon occur, for I know how the planet will end:- I am aware of that. I don't want to frighten anybody but only warn you in time...because the facts will come and there is no time to waste in illusions".

Whatever opinion or interpretation can be made to each of the prophecies, our scientific knowledge is growing daily and we are giving more in-depth scientific data that backs all these prophecies up and dots connect to the exact same outcome.

That is the connection between humans and humans being made in the image of God, the manipulation of DNA that birthed the human race and the some of the connections between the biblical accounts and the Sumerian tablets, according to different translations or researchers. These stories are found throughout history from all different parts of the world in different eras.

CHAPTER 2.

ANUNNAKI, ILLUMINATI AND THE SATANIC TIES.

It is very important to understand how all of this ties to the illuminati, the dark forces that run this planet through their very demonic structure.

According to different sources from various different researchers and independent websites, the illuminati are of the royal bloodline of the enlightened ones, who practice black magic to summon the powers of the underworld, which seems far-fetched to many, however, they use symbology in plain sight.

King Solomon is one of the key figures in understanding how they invoked the powers of the satanic realms, the lower frequencies, the other dimension, which CERN is using also but I'll get to CERN later.

This end times deception study will focus on the hexagram, which we've been told is the

'Star of David', the universally recognised symbol of the state of Israel and the Jews. The truth is that King David never used a star, so calling it the 'Star of David' is a nice sounding name to cover what it really represents.

The Star of David ?

Nowhere in the Bible or the Talmud is this referenced as the Star of David

However, the Bible does reference this to be the Star of Remphan belonging to Moloch (Satan)

Satan hides the true meaning of his symbols behind counterfeit explanations.

To summarise, the six-pointed star is the supreme symbol of Satanic tyranny, which has been used by people throughout history to directly or indirectly worship Satan.

The idolatrous Babylonians, Egyptians and Assyrians used it.

The Israelites worshiped star Gods, such as Remphan and Chiun.

Solomon used it in worship of false Gods and to invoke the powers of Satan.

The Antichrist Beast of Revelation, the Roman Catholic Church, uses it.

The Jesuit-controlled ultra-wealthy Rothchild family uses it to steal the worlds wealth.

Satanists, Luciferians, astrologers and witches use it to invoke the power of demons.

The six-sided star numerically equals 666 (6 points, 6 triangles, 6-sided hexagon). It's on Israel's flag because the Antichrist Jesuits control the state of Israel.

Christians shouldn't have anything to do with the six-pointed star, as it is Satanic.

This 'mark of the beast' identifies people groups that are Antichrist.

The six-sided star was used by Babylonian astrologers for Sun worship. Babylonian astrologers divided the starry heavens into 36 constellations (ten days each). These were represented by different amulets called "Sigilla Solis," or the Sun Seal. These amulets were worn by the pagan priests and they contained all the numbers from 1 to 36. By these figures, they claimed to be able to foretell future events. Adding the numbers of any column either horizontally or vertically, and also the two diagonals crossing the square, the total is the same — 111. The sum of the six columns, either horizontally or vertically, is 666. So 666 is a number associated with pagan sun-worship, which originated in the mysteries of ancient pagan Babylon. Sun worship, which is really Satan worship, has existed for thousands of years and is still worshiped to this very day by Mystery Babylon, the Roman Catholic Church and the global elite in the world.

The Israelites worshiped the star of foreign Gods and were punished for it. Israel adopted the six-pointed star in the wilderness due to their apostasy.

The mark of Cain was worshiped by the Israelites in the wilderness as the star of Remphan, which represents the God Saturn, also called Chiun.

"But ye have borne the tabernacle of your Moloch and Chiun your images, the star of your God, which ye made to yourselves."
Amos 5:-26

Just before being stoned to death by the Jews, Stephen accused the Jewish leaders, *"And you took up the tent of Moloch, and the star of your God Remphan, the figures which you made" "in order to worship them."* Acts 7:43
Saturn worship is Satan worship.
Satan got Solomon to worship him through false Gods.

After his marriage to Pharaoh's daughter in 922 B.C., Solomon gave himself up to witchcraft and idolatry, and built altars to Moloch, Ashtoreth and Remphan, the ancient Egyptian 'Star' God.

This is very significant, because Solomon was a man of wisdom, who was allowed to build the temple of God; yet late in his life Satan caused him to worship and build altars to false Gods, and use the hexagram to invoke the powers of Satan.

King Solomon reintroduced the 6-Pointed Star to the Kingdom of Israel, so the Talisman of Saturn became known as the Seal of Solomon.

The Six-Pointed Star is engraved on the Talisman of Saturn which is used in ritual magic.

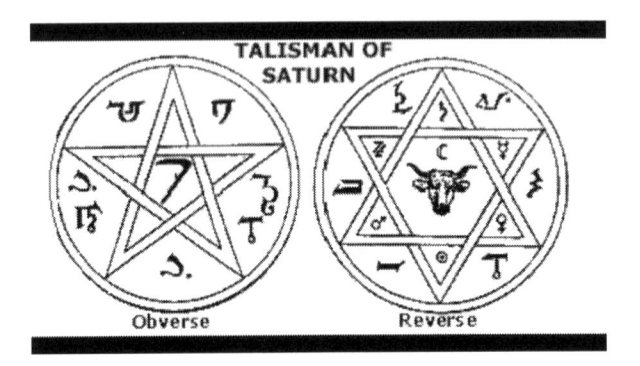

TALISMAN OF SATURN

Obverse / Reverse

A bull's head is enclosed in a six-pointed star, and surrounded by letters composing the name Rempha, the planetary genius of Saturn, according to the alphabet of the Magi.
The bull represents Moloch worship and ultimately, Satan worship.

Satanists, Occultist and Freemasons venerate King Solomon, who owned a magic ring that was engraved with the Seal of Solomon, which gave him power over the invisible monarchy of demons. (The History And Practice Of Magic, Vol. 2)

The six-pointed star represents Satan, not the Star of David.

The Hexagram equates to 666, which according to the bible studies, Jesus said is the sign of the beast.

It has six points, forms six equilateral triangles, and its interior forms a six-sided hexagon — thus it reveals the number of Satan's antichrist beast.

The 6 points, 6 triangles, and the 6 sides of the hexagon = 666

The Bible attributes the number 666 to Solomon.

"Here is wisdom. Let him that hath understanding count the number of the beast:- for it is the number of a man; and his number is SIX HUNDRED THREESCORE AND SIX. "(Rev. 13:-18)
"Now the weight of gold that came to Solomon in one year was SIX HUNDRED THREESCORE AND SIX talents of gold..." (1 Kings 10:-14)

So it was Solomon (not David) who used the Hexagram.

This worship of Satanic false Gods angered God so much, that after Solomon died, God split the kingdom of Israel in two.

The end times False Messiah will no doubt be like a reincarnated Solomon, who unites the world together with his wisdom.

To understand the mark of the beast, you need to know who the beast is first.

If you've read Bible studies, you know that the Roman Catholic Church is the 'Antichrist beast of Revelation', the 'Little Horn of Daniel', and the Pope is the 'Son of Perdition'.

To read a Bible study on the beasts of Daniel and Revelation that reveals the antichrist beast system; look out for the Bible study of how the Antichrist Roman Catholic Church is already seated in the temple and proclaiming to be God; look out for Antichrist In The Temple Deception.

Is the hexagram the symbol that Satan will use as the Mark of the Beast? As you will see, it makes sense, because it's a symbol that's already accepted by almost every religion.

In the New World Order they will promote a one-world religion in the name of 'peace', so they will use a symbol that will unite the major religions, and the so-called Star of David is the perfect mark.

When Christians speculate about the Mark of the Beast, they point to UPC codes, implanted RFID chips, RFID tattoos, and other technology.

While there's no doubt that those type of devices will be used to control whether people can buy or sell in the one-world government and financial system. Receiving the Mark of the Beast is a RESULT of worshiping the image of the beast.

Revelation 13:15 says, *"He was granted power to give breath to the image of the beast, that the image of the beast should both speak and cause as many as would not worship the image of the beast to be killed."*

When you refuse to 'worship the image of the beast', you will be killed by the beast, or will be prevented from buying and selling.

According to the bible, when you profess your allegiance to Jesus, even in the face of death, then you will have eternal life. *"And they overcame him by the blood of the Lamb and by the word of their testimony, and they did not love their lives to the death."* Rev. 12:11

If you 'worship the image of the beast' in order to preserve your life, then you will incur the wrath of God.

Revelation 13:17 says, *"and that no one may buy or sell except one who has the mark or the name of the beast, or the number of his name."*

The Jesuits are the Earth beast of Revelation 13, which will enforce the mark of the beast. The Jesuits control all of the world's financial organisations, such as the World Bank, the International Monetary Fund, and the International Bank of Settlements; the Central Banks of almost every country in the world, such as the U.S. Federal Reserve Bank; and they control the major banks and financial institutions, such as Citibank and Goldman Sachs.

They control all of this through their city-state City of London corporation.

So they will be able to regulate who buys and sells in the New World Order.

So your eternal destiny primarily depends on whether you will kneel and worship the Antichrist beast system. Taking the mark of the beast is a result of worshiping the beast.

If you believe that you will be 'raptured' out before the tribulation period, and that you won't have to face the beast system, you definitely want to read the Bible study called The Pre-Tribulation Rapture Myth.

The mark will identify which people belong to the beast, as it will clearly show that they are subject to its authority.

The Jews in Germany had to wear a star on the outside of their clothes, so that they were easily identified. The hexagram represents Satan worship. Satan ever seeks to establish his worship among the Earth.

According to bible studies, he even tempted Jesus to bow down and worship him. How much more will he lead people in the end times, either through deceit or enticement, to do the same?

Most people aren't going to worship Satan directly, so he uses other 'Gods' and 'idols', to accept worship indirectly.

Throughout the Middle Ages, the Seal of Solomon has been used by Arab Magicians, Cabalist Magicians, Druid witches and Satanists.

THE GREAT SYMBOL OF SOLOMON

It's the most powerful symbol used to invoke witchcraft, demons and Satan. It's used in magic, witchcraft, sorcery, occultism, alchemy and the casting of zodiacal horoscopes by astrologers.

In fact, the word 'hex', as in to put a hex on someone, derives from the word hexagram. According to former Satanist Bill Schnoebelen, who is now a Christian, *"a hexagram must be present to call forth a demon" and "it is a very powerful tool to invoke Satan."*

It is no mystery that in all the occults, the hex plays a central role in Satan worship and upon and within these covens, human sacrifices are offered to Satan.

The hexagram, like the pentagram, is used in practices of the occult and ceremonial magic and is attributed to the 7 "old" planets outlined in astrology.

The symbol is linked with sun worship and the sun God which again links back to the Mystery Religions.

Deuteronomy 4:19 *says "And beware, lest you lift up your eyes to heaven and see the sun and the moon and the stars, all the host of heaven, and be drawn away and worship them and serve them."*

The Satanic Illuminati offers sacrifices to Satan on his revered days, which are based on the cycles of the Sun. 3/21 - A human sacrifice is required on the Spring equinox. 4/19 - A fire sacrifice and a human sacrifice is to be made to the Beast. Note:- the Oklahoma City bombing and the Waco Branch Davidian siege occurred on this date.

6/21 - A human sacrifice is required on the summer solstice, which is called Litha.

9/21 - A human sacrifice is required on the fall equinox, which is called Mabon.

12/21 - A human sacrifice is required on the winter solstice, which is called Yule.

Luciferians revere the hexagram. Luciferians don't use the name Satan. They believe that Lucifer is the good God, and that the God of the Bible is the evil God.

Helena Blavatsky wrote that *"Lucifer is the true God"*, and she incorporated the hexagram in the emblem of the Theosophical Society, which she founded in 1875.

The six-sided star is prominent in their emblem, which includes the Swastika, the Ankh(cross with a circle that represents eternal life), the Aum, and the Ouroboros (an ancient symbol depicting a serpent or dragon eating its own tail.). She believed *that "There is no religion higher than (Lucifer's) truth."*
"The interlaced triangles, one (lighter) pointing upwards and the other (darker) pointing downwards, symbolise the descent of spirit into matter and its emergence from the confining limits of form. At the same time they suggest the constant conflict between light and dark forces in nature and man. When, as in the emblem, the double triangle is depicted within the circle of the Serpent, the whole of manifested nature is represented, the universe bounded by the limitations of time and space."

Aleister Crowley was a terribly decadent, heroin-addicted, bisexual Satan worshiper, who asked people to call *him "The Beast 666."*

Crowley believed that he was literally the antimessiah of the apocalypse. He founded the Satanic order of the Silver Star and he designed the unicursal hexagram. His satanic motto was *"Do what thou wilt shall be the whole of the Law."*

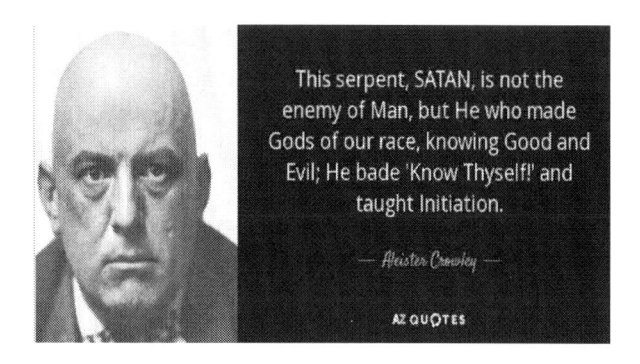

> This serpent, SATAN, is not the enemy of Man, but He who made Gods of our race, knowing Good and Evil; He bade 'Know Thyself!' and taught Initiation.
>
> — Aleister Crowley

Based on those associations, you shouldn't support anything using the symbol. The beast of Revelation, the Roman Catholic Church, uses the hexagram.

The Antichrist Roman Catholic Church reveres the symbol, and every entity that they control uses it too. This includes the Rothschild family, Freemasonry, Zionism, the state of Israel, and false religions, the Satanic Hexagram prominently placed on the Pope's mitre. The mitre is shaped like a fish mouth, representing Dagon, the Babylonian fish-God. In the mystery religions, both the forehead and hands were tattooed during rites of initiation, to honour Dagon whose hands and head were cut off by God. Read 1 Samuel 5:1-5

Now think about where the mark of the beast will be placed, on the forehead and hand, just as in the Mystery Religions.

"No one will enter the New World Order unless he or she will make a pledge to worship Lucifer. No one will enter the New Age unless he will take a Luciferian Initiation." - David Spangler, Director of Planetary Initiative, United Nations.

The state of St. Peter at the Vatican features a Satanic hexagram. This statue of Peter at the Vatican features the supposed keys to the church and a disguised hexagram. Most people wouldn't notice the six points, which form the hexagram. The Roman Catholic Church falsely claims that the church was founded by Peter the Apostle.

The Satanic hexagram could not represent the true church. And according to the bible studies, Jesus told us in Revelation that 666 represents the Antichrist beast.

This Pope's Monstrance features a hexagram surrounded by a Sun symbol. The hexagram is disguised, as most people don't understand the meaning of the six points on this monstrance. It clearly forms a hexagram, and it has the wafer, the supposed body of Christ, right in the middle of the Satanic symbol. The hexagram is a curse mark, so in essence, this is cursing the body of Christ.

St. John Cantius Church in the Archdiocese of Chicago features a hexagram, a hexagram with the Chi-Rho symbol in the middle. It is on the floor of the St. John Cantius Church in the Archdiocese of Chicago.

The Roman Catholic Church Chi-Rho symbol represents the hexagram. The Chi-Rho was the Mark of the Roman Empire. It has six points which form a hexagram. The Roman Catholic Church uses the Chi-Rho symbol, as an alternative to the hexagram.

The Jesuit-controlled Rothschild family uses the Hexagram. The Rothschild family is controlled by the Jesuits, who are the covert military arm of the Roman Catholic Church.

In the 17th century, the family changed their last name from Bauer to Rothschild, which means 'red-shield', as family patriarch Mayer Amschel Bauer began hanging out a red hexagram in front of their house to identify it. The red hexagram was patterned after the red Seal of Solomon. The Rothschild's are Satanists who used this powerful magic symbol in their coat-of-arms.

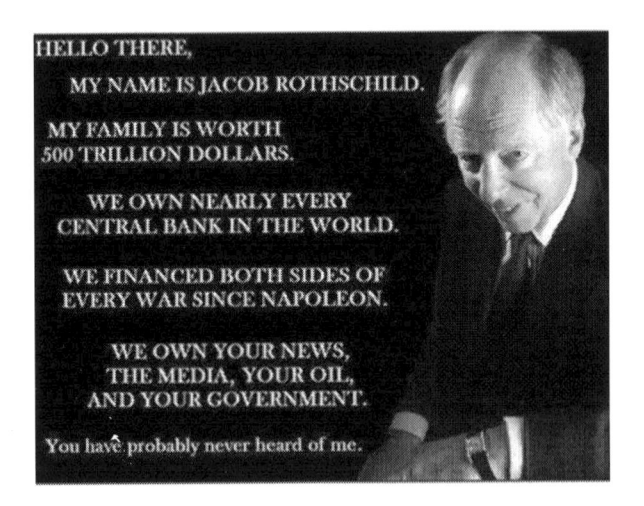

HELLO THERE,
   MY NAME IS JACOB ROTHSCHILD.

MY FAMILY IS WORTH
500 TRILLION DOLLARS.

   WE OWN NEARLY EVERY
CENTRAL BANK IN THE WORLD.

   WE FINANCED BOTH SIDES OF
EVERY WAR SINCE NAPOLEON.

   WE OWN YOUR NEWS,
   THE MEDIA, YOUR OIL,
   AND YOUR GOVERNMENT.

You have probably never heard of me.

Since 1823, the Rothschilds have controlled the vast financial holdings of the Roman Catholic Church. The Rothschild family is ultra-wealthy because their banking schemes have stolen the wealth of the nations, including the U.S. via the Federal Reserve Bank.

They are gathering the world's wealth, so that they can control the one-world monetary system. They have hundreds of trillions of dollars, and they control the International Monetary Fund, the World Bank, the International Bank of Settlements in Switzerland, and the central banks of nearly every county in the world.

The compass of Freemasonry represents a hexagram. The Jesuit-controlled Illuminati infiltrated the order of Freemasonry to use it as a front-organisation, to promote their Satanic agenda to create a New World Order. The hexagram shape is hidden in their compass and ruler design, and on their temples. At the lower levels, Freemasons are not made aware of the Satanic secret society. At the 32nd and 33rd degrees of Freemasonry, their God is revealed as Lucifer the light-bearer. The six-pointed "Blazing Star" points to the true deity they worship, Lucifer.

Sacred Society

Through the Freemasons, the evil elite draw in the best people in society, and promote the ones who conform to their will. This helps them build levels of control, as these people run corporations and governments.

King Solomon is the most important figure in Freemasonry, because he fell away from God and worshiped false Gods, and he used the six-sided star to invoke the powers of Satan.

We all know the illuminati and their agenda, it goes very deep and is a very well organised cult that literally run the whole planet, from the food we eat to the clothes that we wear, they control the banking systems, they control the politicians, they control who lives and who dies in the music industry, they literally control it all.

Satan/baphomet/Horus/lucifer/nimrod (well there are many names) but that is who they worship. They serve Satan and that's why all the music videos the woman are inappropriately dancing in a cube or triangle/have lightning bolts in the video/covering one eye and many more ritualistic symbolism.

Now to give you an idea of how well organised they are you have to look for the things hidden in plain sight like Christmas, believe it or not is actually a celebration and massive worldwide ritual to the birth of Tammuz (Anti-Christ) so you can imagine how far back this was all planned and put together, literally drummed in to everyone that it's a celebration of Christ, that's how they work, everything is an inversion of Christ so it's a mockery to Christ and it's absolutely everywhere in front of you, it's literally exactly what they said it would be in the bible 'age of deception'.

You may hear all the time about 'the golden age' well again this is actually the 'golden age of lucifer' like the new world order as such, one world religion/government, said that in the bible too.

The Catholic Church was infiltrated by the illuminati years and years ago and gradually changed parts of the bible to suit their agenda, that's why outside the Vatican near Christmas Day, they have all the plastic models out pretending that it's depicting the birth of Christ when in reality they are paying respects to the birth of Tammuz in the secret chambers whilst immigrants are trying to get in but to the people going to look at the life size models are none the wiser and they just think it's actually the birth of Jesus, it's not. They have literally deceived the whole world just like it says in the bible, once you piece it all together you'll understand the day and age we are living in 'the golden age'/ 'self ascension' (selfies/wanting money/trying to be famous/breast implants/lip fillers) it's all me, me, me these days i.e. Self ascension, again- said it would happen in the bible.

Illuminati=Satan=Saturn worship=black sun=black cube of Saturn and it's all around you daily in plain sight.

Even the Catholic chalice has the letters **IHS** in the centre and this means SIS/HORUS/SET Egyptian Gods/Anti-Christ and the three nails that Jesus was crucified with (inversion of Christ) so it's so deep guys trust me nearly every church out there has been infiltrated and has Anti-Christ symbolism everywhere like golden Phoenix's (rise of the Phoenix, Satan) or depictions of the birth of Tammuz, not Jesus.

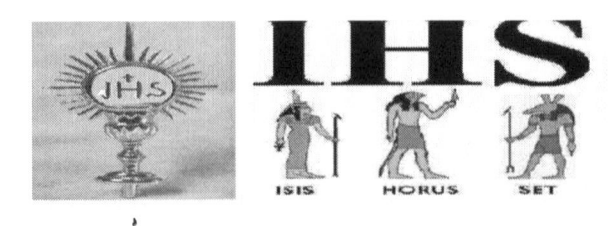

The 'all seeing eye' is also a very symbolic gesture in the elitist illuminati/Masonic agenda.

Osiris had a son Horus who is referred to by the Egyptians as the "morning Star", the hieroglyphic for this means divine wisdom. Egyptian kings were thought to be an incarnation of Horus, this was passed from father to son upon death. Where upon he merges and becomes one with Osiris.

A passage from the Pyramid Texts shows that the new Horus was considered to be the morning star, when the new Osiris says:- *'The reed-floats of the sky are set in place for me, that I may cross by means of them to Ra at the horizon. ...I will stand among them, for the moon is my brother, the Morning Star is my offspring...'... the Egyptian hieroglyphic for the morning star has the literal meaning 'divine knowledge'."* (The Hiram Key, Knight & Lomas)

This brings new meaning to highly honoured Freemason Albert Pike's often quoted verse:-

Illuminati pyramid and '33' Means 33rd degree mason

Pheonix - rise of the Phoenix lucifer

Hexagram (devil worship)

"Lucifer, the Light-bearer! Strange and mysterious name to give to the Spirit of Darkness! Lucifer, the Son of the Morning!" Just a different interpretation. As always.

"Everything good in nature comes from OSIRIS - order, harmony, and the favourable temperature of the seasons and celestial periods." (page 476 - The Lost Keys of Freemasonry, Manly P. Hall, 33rd, page 65,

Macoy Publishing and Masonic Supply Co. Richmond, Va., 1976)

In 1880, Kenneth Anger, Kenneth Anger, a follower of the "founding father" of modern Satanism, Aleister Crowley, produced a film called "Lucifer Rising", in which he portrays Lucifer as a beautiful bringer of light and a cosmic trickster. The music for the film was produced by Bobby Beausoleil, who was a sidekick of the serial killer and Satanist, Charles Manson. "Lucifer Rising" was filmed in Luxor, Karnak, Gizeh, Externsteine, London and Avebury. Mick Jagger (one of his squeezes was Maianne Faithful, who played Lilith in the film) was evidently taken with Anger's work (indeed Anger claims it was their conversations which inspired Jagger to write "Sympathy for the Devil") and agreed to take the part of Lucifer. He backed down before shooting began, however, apparently fearing that the Satanic aura he had once sought to cultivate was becoming to tangible for comfort. Eventually a Middlesbrough steel worker named Leslie Huggins was recruited for the part.

Kenneth anger, he wrote of lucifer- *"Like SCORPIO RISING, LUCIFER RISING is about several things. I'm an artist working in*

Light, and that's my whole interest, really. Lucifer is the Light God, not the devil, that's a Christian Slander... I'm showing actual ceremonies in the film; what is performed in front of the camera won't be a re-enactment and purpose will be to make Lucifer Rise... Lucifer is the Rebel Angel behind what's happening in the world today."

The ascension of Lucifer (Horus), Bringer of Light, invoked by Isis, Osiris, Lucifer's Adept, Lilith and the Magus.

the adepts of the concealed inner Temple, tell us that Horus is really Lucifer and that the coming NWO, the Masonic version of the Aquarian Age, is synonymous with the age of Horus. The Masonic Horus/Lucifer one and the same. Anger was affiliated with Anton LaVey's Church of Satan as well... and Of course Horus is Lucifer and the eye of Horus on the Dollar bill is the eye of Satan.

Osiris, both King of the Egyptians and their God, went on a long journey to bless neighbouring nations with his knowledge of arts and sciences. His jealous brother, Typhon (God of Winter AKA Set) conspired to murder him, steal his kingdom and did so. Isis, sister and wife of Osiris and his queen (as well as Egypt's Moon-Goddess) set out on a search for the body, making inquiries of all she met. Again, all interpretations of the bible just changed in certain aspects to mislead people, if you know the ancient texts then the bible is more understandable.

This is in extremely abbreviated form, is the Egyptian legend of Isis and Osiris. It is without doubt, the basis for the Masonic legend of Hiram Abiff.

Each sincere man who is initiated into the Third (Master Mason) Degree of Masonry impersonates Osiris, the Sun-God of Egypt, and enters into his life of good deeds, his death, his burial and is "raised" in his resurrection from the dead. With this understood, it is then easy to understand the statement in the Kentucky Monitor (handbook for all Blue Lodge Masonry in the Grand Lodge of Kentucky) that, while the Christian's Messiah is called Jesus, the Mason's Messiah is called Hiram (Kentucky Monitor, "the Spirit of Masonry," xv) same story of Osiris.

All-Seeing Eye features prominently in Jean-Jacques-François Le Barbier's 1789 representation of the Declaration of the Rights of Man and of the Citizen. For many, the symbol is further proof that the Illuminati was the hidden forces behind the French revolution.

In an episode titled Cephalopod Lodge, SpongeBob SquarePants and his starfish buddy (Patrick Star) infiltrate a Masonic-like Lodge called the Cephalopod Lodge. The Lodge building itself is shaped like a pyramid. The capstone opens to eject any Cowan infiltrators.

Then you have a triangle with a circle in it is used as the Sign of the Deathly Hallows in the Harry Potter universe. The Sign of the Deathly Hallows is a triangular mark used as a representation of the Deathly Hallows, three legendary objects that allegedly, if united, would make one the "Master of Death".

Then Ducktales the Movie:- Treasure of the Lost Lamp Pyramid is a 1990 Disney animated film. Disney does not consider it part of its canon of animated feature films despite being released in theatres yet you can clearly see a golden pyramid with the all seeing eye at the capstone.

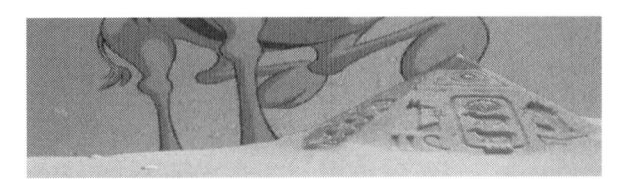

Even MI5, you know the British intelligence agency charged with domestic affairs. One of the its early logo features an All-Seeing Eye embedded in the capstone of a pyramid.

Even the Supreme Court Building, it has a huge pyramid with a huge circular hole surrounding it which depicts the all seeing eye, located in Jerusalem and was donated to Israel by Dorothy de Rothschild, wife of James Armand de Rothschild of the French banking dynasty.

The Ukrainian ₴500 Hryvnia note features an all-seeing eye within a triangle on the back.

The US one dollar bill also includes an all-seeing eye in a triangle floating atop an unfinished pyramid.

Miley Cyrus was a former Disney Musketeer and starred in Hannah Montana, a popular American teen sitcom on the Disney Channel. Disney is said to have close ties to the 13 Illuminati families and author such as Fritz Springmeier specifically mentions Disney's theme parks as sites for Illuminati Mind Control programming.

Some researchers believe that former
Mousketeers such as Cyrus, Britney Spears,

Christina Aguilera, Selena Gomez, and Justin Timberlake are Monarch mind-control slaves:- well if you know the truth then you'll know that this is spot on.

Eminem doing the Devil's Horns hand sign on artwork associated with his The Marshall Mathers LP 2. (I haven't seen any album which included the artwork)

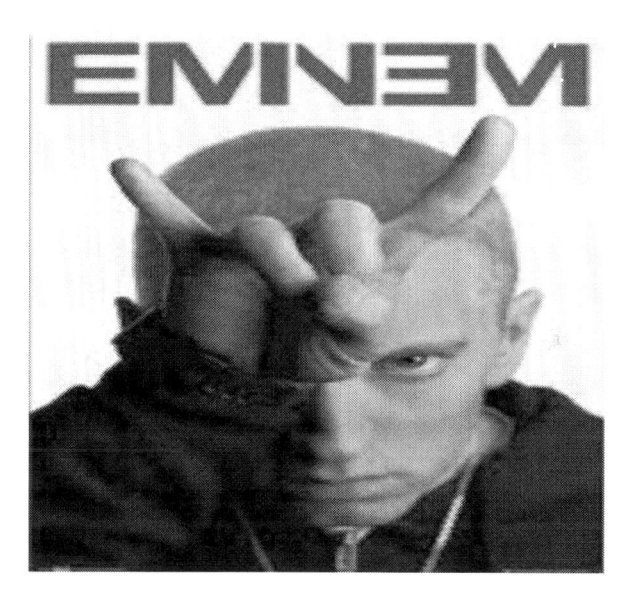

The Devil's Horns or El Diablo is said to be a hand gesture saluting Satan. Illuminati researchers know this. Hence the wine-

In order to achieve success, musicians must first make a sacrifice and pledge their souls to Satan i.e. Sell your soul for money and power and sacrifice a family member (Kanye West sacrificed his own mother) then people like Lady Gaga does the Hidden Eye sign repeatedly in her music video, Just Dance. The Hidden Eye, or more importantly, the one exposed eye, represent the All-Seeing eye of the Illuminati which you probably understand by now.

Naomi Campbell, on her 41st birthday got given from Russian billionaire ex-boyfriend Vladislav Doronin "Cleopatra Island" in Gulf of Turkey A house is shaped like the ' Eye of Horus'.

NAOMI CAMPBELL'S HORUS-EYE ECO HOUSE

The combination of the All-Seeing Eye floating in a capstone over a 13-step unfinished pyramid is the most popular Illuminati symbols and by far the most recognisable symbol of the Illuminati.

The eye represents the Illuminati ruling from their position on the capstone of the pyramid. There are very few at the top while we are many at the bottom.

The all-seeing eye on the pyramid was added to the reverse side of the Great Seal of the United States and finally adopted by Congress in 1782. In 1935, President and 33rd degree Freemason, Franklin Roosevelt added the front and back of the Seal to the one dollar bill.

The All-Seeing Eye floating is representative of the Illuminati seeing themselves as Gods, and being able to see and watch everything that we do. They are rapidly approaching their goals thanks to quickly advancing technology,

technologies is one of the greatest weapons that Lucifer has.

The pyramid represents the command structure of the Illuminati with very few people commanding from the capstone. The 13-step pyramid found on the US dollar bill represents the 13 families of the Illuminati. These are the direct descendants of the Anunnaki blood line and the ones that see themselves as the Gods of the Earth.

Basic Illuminati Pyramid Structure

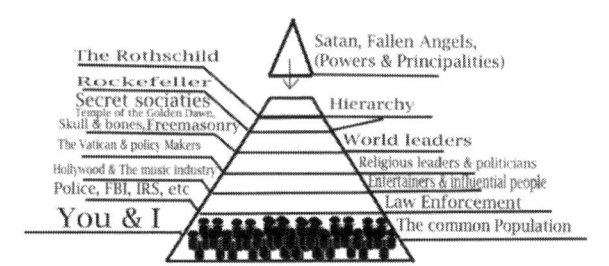

Left side	Right side
The Rothschild	Satan, Fallen Angels, (Powers & Principalities)
Rockefeller	
Secret societies — Temple of the Golden Dawn, Skull & bones, Freemasonry	Hierarchy
The Vatican & policy Makers	World leaders
Hollywood & The music industry	Religious leaders & politicians / Entertainers & influential people
Police, FBI, IRS, etc	Law Enforcement
You & I	The common Population

The inverted pentagram or reversed pentagram with two points up is a symbol of evil. It represents a Goat of Mendes attacking heaven with its horns pointing upwards. It is also known as the Sign of the Cloven Hoof, or Footprint of the Devil. Which is why it's featured in certain military regiments.

The lightning bolts represent Lucifer, the fallen angel, falling from heaven as a lightning bolt as described in Luke 18:-10. The lightning bolt is a Satanic ray widely used in the music industry. This again means the Anunnaki coming down from the heavens, this is the fallen angels described in the bible which is just an interpretation of the Sumerian tablets.

Snakes usually represent temptation as represented in the Garden of Eden. The snake traditionally imparts forbidden knowledge which is used as a lure by the Illuminati. Serpents are seen in the Ouroboros and caduceus symbols. Again; this is just an interpretation of the two snakes of the manipulation of DNA found in the ancient Sumerian tablets. The serpent swallowing its own tail represents infinity. The symbol reinforces the Illuminati's perception that they are immortal and eternal like Gods because they carry on their bloodlines and live a lot longer than the average human. This is why all the celebrities in the music industry pledge their allegiance through symbolic tattoos.

The eagle (Phoenix) is a symbol or power and endurance. The Romans, The House of Habsburg, The House of Rothschild, the Nazis, and the United States all used the eagle as a symbol. See the ravenous bird from the east from Isaiah 46:-11 another interpretation from the Sumerian tablets reproduced in the bible. This is why the church's in modern history have alters where they read from a golden Phoenix. Here's a few examples of how satanic the churches have become; see if you can spot the blatant symbolism-

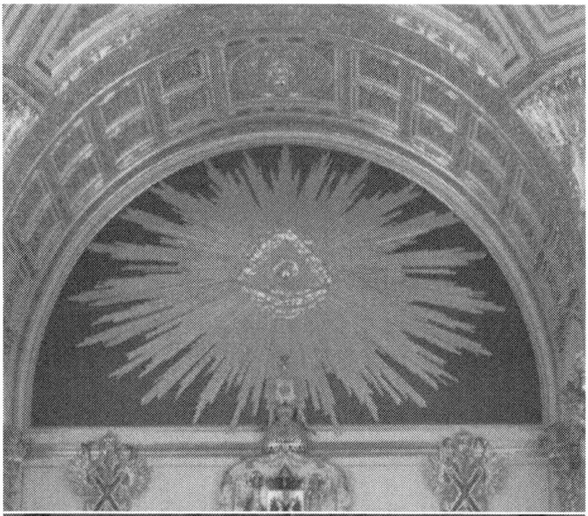

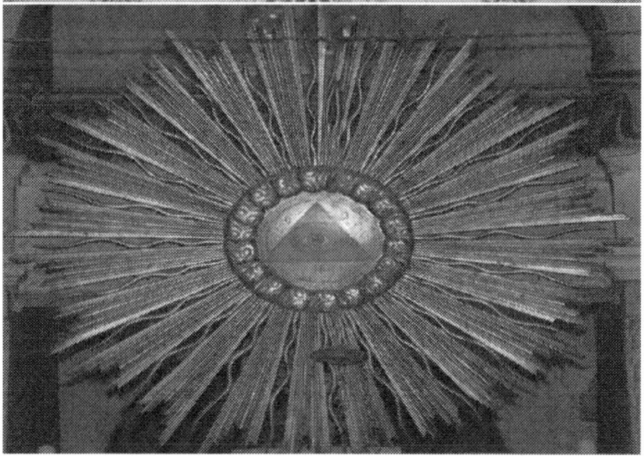

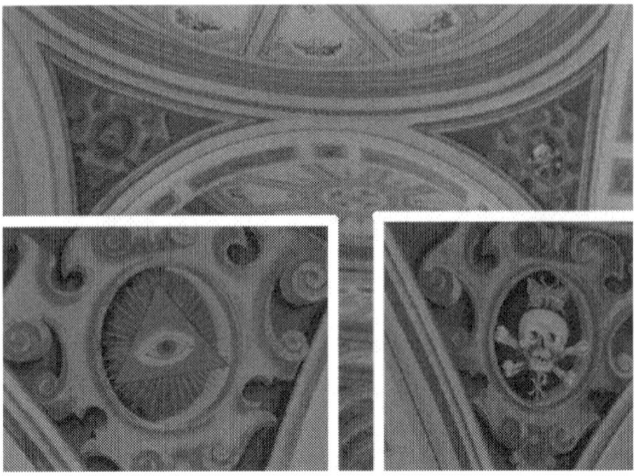

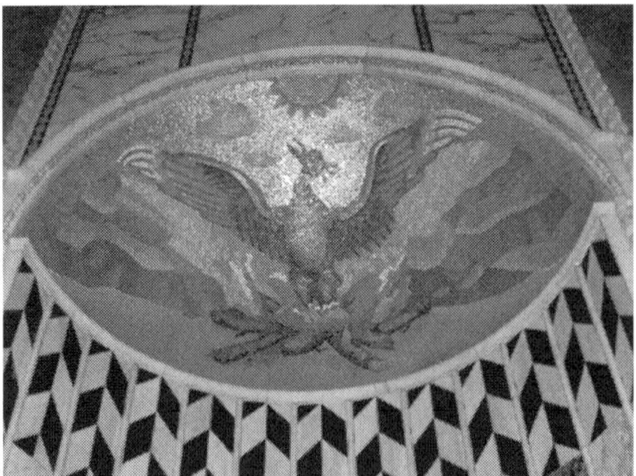

Now look at London fashion week in 2017, what can you see?

Skulls are used as a reminder of death in Freemasonry and for the Skull and Bones. Young initiates are reminded that they only have a short life to work towards the eternal Illuminati's goals.

Also known as the Sign of Hermetism, to the Illuminati, it represents the destruction of Earth and civilisation. With the bringing of chaos, Earth is to become like Hell – As Above, So Below.

The eye of Horus originated from Egypt and originated from 'the white brotherhood' which all started from the Anunnaki, creator of man, the fallen angels, as depicted in the bible.

The Anunnaki saw themselves as Gods and went against the creator when in reality they were just a more advanced civilisation which altered our DNA to make us slaves to this planet to mine for gold for their purposes, as stated above.

Not Gods, just races. all part of the deception to worship them as Gods through power/magic/sorcery so we look to them as if they are Gods.

The contrast between the black and white squares represents the duality between good and evil. The checkered floor is in all Masonic Lodges.

The mirror, especially when cracked or shattered, is an important and reoccurring symbol in Monarch programming. Each broken shard represents a different personality, or alter programmed by handlers in mind control slaves. Also represents the cracking open of time and space, like CERN are trying to do with opening dimensions. This is why the music industry uses mirrors in their videos.

The Order of the Eastern Star is a Masonic organisation which allows women to participate in some Masonic-related activities. Women are specifically forbidden to join regular Masonic Lodge. There are about half a million members of the Order throughout the world.

The logo for the General Grand Chapter includes an inverted pentagram. The five points of the pentagram represent the five Biblical heroines Adah, Ruth, Esther, Martha, and Electa.

Birdcage is symbolism of imprisonment, used in Monarch mind-control programming. The symbols are a literal representation of the mental and physical bondage of Illuminati slaves. They have these bird cages in all Rothschild dinner parties and is very apparent in the demonic music industry-

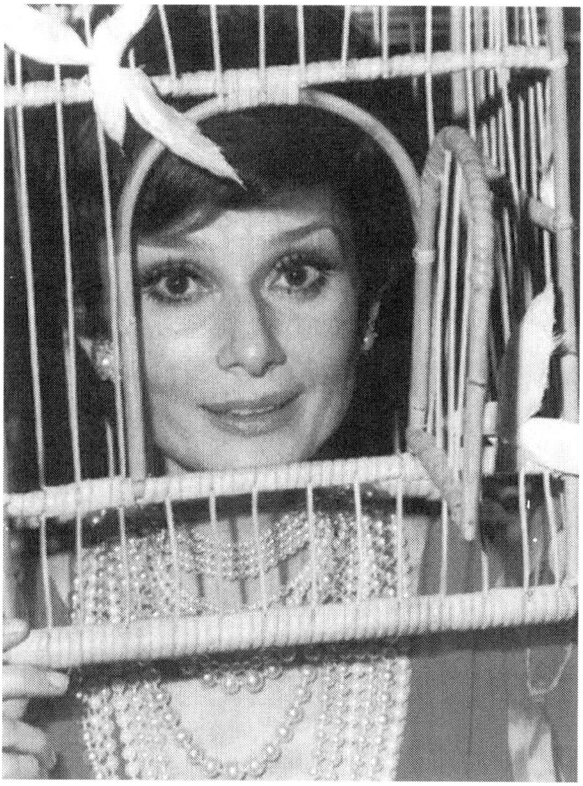

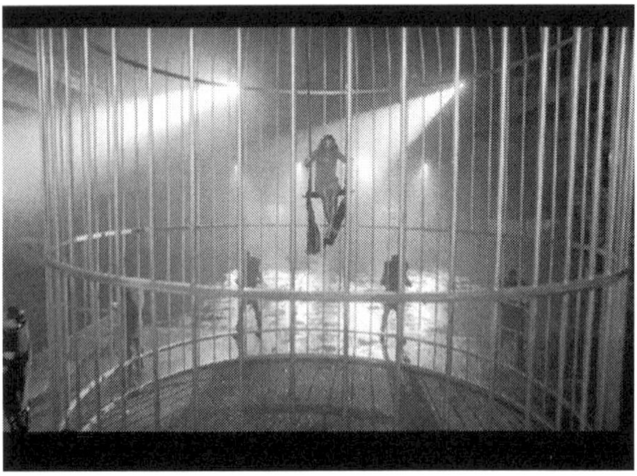

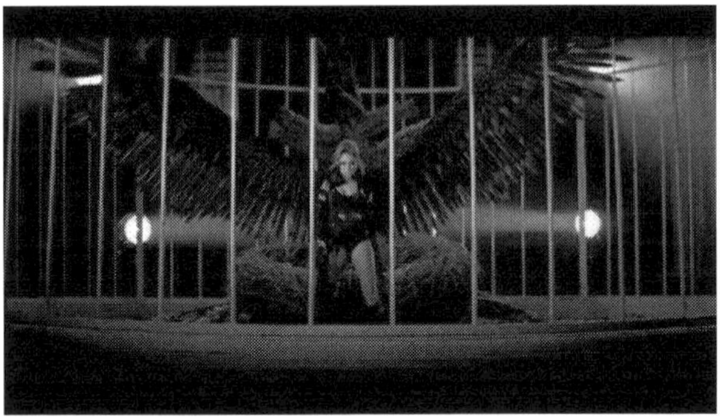

The Bavarian Illuminati was active in Bavaria at the end of the 18th century, it then went underground and continue to operate behind the scene to this very day with families such as the Rockefeller's and Rothschilds leading the way until they managed to brainwash the masses.

Jesus had a conscience that wasn't from the Anunnaki, he was more connected to the universe through the highest frequency of all 'love', so he was the son of Our good creation, the universe itself, sent here to warn us of their doings and agendas, yes, the elite worships the Anunnaki as Gods because they are rewarded with power and wealth, we are a creation of a better race but they did not create our bonding soul, that's Gods work, that's an inter dimensional race, our spiritual world if you will. That's the whole deception that's plagued this Earth, we bow down to the race that made us slaves when we should be free.

So what I'm getting at here is that the eye of Horus is used in lots of different ways by lots of different cultures but it all represents the same thing- deception.

They all use the symbolism for worship and power to the false Gods, yet people will believe they are Gods because of the power they hold and the power they can give.

In reality they are all worshippers of the negative realm, this is what's been hidden from the public for centuries and have manipulated the masses into believing that their is no creator, it was all one Big Bang, a huge coincidence that birthed life in a complex form, That's how they work.

The good tried to warn us that God has no cravings of our flesh/body for he did not create us to be full of pride/power/self ascension, he gave Satan reign over Earth as it's not a fight for flesh and blood, it's a fight for each person to stay true to their self and be pure in their own soul.

I am in no way pushing religion on to any of you here, I am not religious, I am spiritual. Religion was created to wage wars and form control. Your spirituality is what makes you who you are. You are not born with any religion, you are taught it. You are not born a racist, you are taught it. It's your own 'free will' to how you react to them teachings, we all know right from wrong, we all know good from evil. Choose the good. All I can do is show you how they work.

Many ancient scriptures/carvings all have a similar storyline:-

Anu, Enki, Enlil.

Isis, Horus, Set.

Nimrod, Semiramis, Tammuz.

Abraham, Mary, Jesus.

One thing that they all have in common is that they all originated from one initial story that has carried on through the ages.

Some of the scriptures cannot be manipulated due to them being bonded through the universal law of 'truth'.

Certain texts have been added and said differently to suit certain agendas, the King James Bible was heavily influenced by the Roman Empire in the 1600s and even forced the face of '**Cesaer** Borgia' as Jesus Christ and is the most common image used in modern day societies.

So as you can see, the slavery system that was created in the Anunnaki story still remains today just through different forms; money, power and greed, they have manipulated the minds of the masses to make them believe the materialistic things are of worth whist making you forget your spiritual nature. This is how the negative forces work.

CHAPTER 3

CERN, HAARP, GWEN TOWERS, CHEMTRAILS CONNECTION.

It's important to understand that the pole shift and CERN have the greatest connection, everything that happens on this planet is connected to the pole shift.

First, we must understand the grounds in which the large hadron collider is situated on. Straddling the French-Swiss border, the £8 billion CERN collider complex is buried at a depth of up to 575 feet (175 meters). The tunnel complex runs along a 17-mile (27-kilometer) circuit.

but notice that the town in France where CERN is partially situated is called "Saint-Genus-Poilly." The name Pouilly comes from the Latin "Appolliacum" and it is believed that in Roman times a temple existed in honour of Apollo, and the people who lived there believed that it is a gateway to the underworld.

It is interesting to note that CERN is built on the same spot. Religious leaders, the good kind, are always suspicious of the aims of the scientific world, which draws a connection to a verse straight out of Revelations (9:-1-2, 11), which makes reference to the name 'Apollyon.' The verse states:- *"To him was given the key of the bottomless pit. And he opened the bottomless pit... And they had a kind over them, which is the angel of the bottomless pit, whose name in the Hebrew tongue is Abaddon, but in the Greek tongue hath his name Apollyon."* Yes, you can't make it up. Truth is always stranger that fiction.

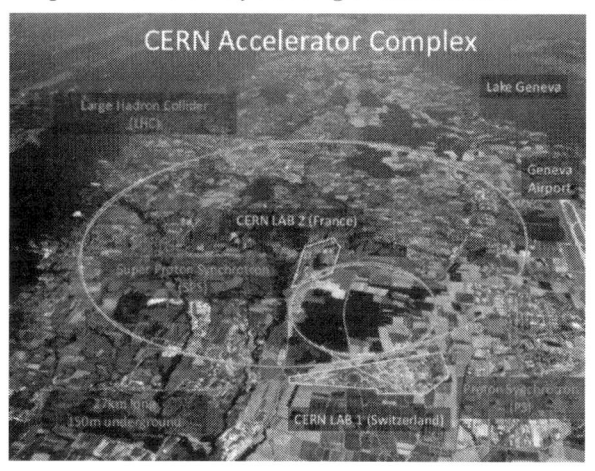

CERN logo also represents 666 hidden in plain sight, just like Disney. All work for the same people:-

The elite always have to show you what they are about in plain sight, this is how they work, the best form of secrecy is to be as blatant as possible which not only subliminally makes your mind except it as normal but also it is their way of sticking to the universal law of 'truth'. Which is why the first 'in your face' clue is in the actually name 'CERN'

The name CERN - 'officially' is the European Organisation for Nuclear Research. The name CERN is derived from the acronym for the French Conseil Européen pour la Recherche Nucléaire, a provisional body founded in 1952 with the mandate of establishing a world-class fundamental physics research organisation animation in Europe.

However, CERN has a very deeper meaning, as always, the elite like to pledge allegiance through ritualistic names and Gods of the underworld, CERN is short for 'cernunnos' who is known in Celtic polytheism as the 'horned God', God of fertility, life, animals, wealth, and the underworld. Which all represent 'flesh and power'. Nothing to do with your spirituality.

It is said that 'cernunnos' is the great hunter, He was known as the most ancient and powerful Celtic deity who was called the "lord of wild and all things." His sons were said to be Teutates, Esus, Taranis or Taranus who are sometimes referred to as his doubles.

The meaning of Cernunnos in Gaelic and Old English and Irish is the "horned one or he who has horns." This God was usually depicted in artwork wearing stag antlers and was normally accompanied by his symbols of the stag, ram, bull and holding a horned and spotted serpent or worm.

The earliest known depictions of Cernunnos were found at Val Camonica, in northern Italy, which was under Celtic occupation from about 400 BC. The most famous was also portrayed on the Gundestrup Caldron (pictured above), which is a silver ritual vessel found at Gundestrup in Jutland, Denmark and dating to about the 1st century BC.

The name "Jutland" would correspond with the Tribe of Judah who are also known as the Phoenicians and Greek Hellenes from Crete who has been written about extensively in articles such as the "First Jews of Crete" and

"The Masonic Archons of the Tribe of Judah" which is always worth reading.

The horned God is found on the famous Pillar of the Boatmen (French Pilier des nautes) is a square-section stone bas-relief with depictions of several deities, both Gaulish and Roman. Dating to the first quarter of the 1st century AD, it originally stood in a temple in the Gallo-Roman civitas of Lutetia (modern Paris, France).

As most of you know now, after reading previous chapters, the great hunter, the bull, the stag, the Ram, the serpent directly ties to the occult. Nimrod being the great hunter, the king who rebelled against God. Nimrod is the father of 'Tammuz' and his wife was 'Semiramis'. Tammuz was born on the 25th of December and the elite have managed to indoctrinate people into creating a worldwide ritual based celebration on that day. This is how they work, hidden in plain sight, fooled the masses, as they always do.

The 'Ram' represents 'baphomet' which is a very used symbolic image within the occult/elite. Since 1856, the name Baphomet has been associated with a "Sabbatic Goat" image drawn by Eliphas Levi which contains binary elements representing the "sum total of the universe". As always, the like to play with minds. 'As above, so below' is them using the Hegelian dialect, good vs evil, the continuous battle.

The bull, the serpent. I mean, I think you get the picture of who they worship.

Then we have to take a delve into the CERN 'mascot' which is the Goddess 'Shiva'. Shiva is the third God in the Hindu triumvirate. The triumvirate consists of three Gods who are responsible for the creation, upkeep and destruction of the world. The other two Gods are Brahma and Vishnu.

Brahma is the creator of the universe while Vishnu is the preserver of it.

"SHIVA's" role is to DESTROY the universe in order to RE-CREATE it. which they are doing in a sense, they are smashing particles of the universe together to recreate the birth of the universe in a contained environment, well that's what they say they are doing, what they are actually doing is much worse.

So Just outside of its headquarters building sits an ancient statue of Shiva, ancient Apollyon, the Goddess of destruction. Strange? Not when you know how they work. Connect the dots.

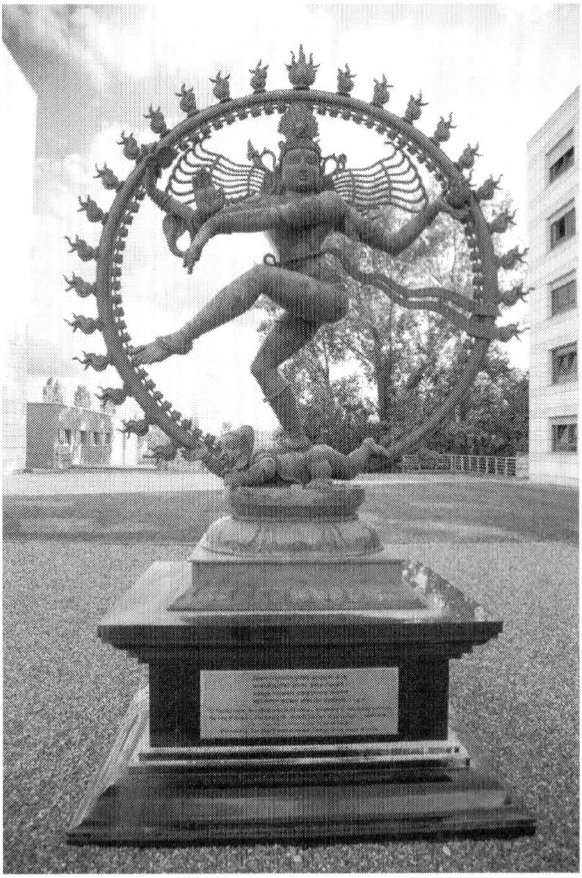

GOD OF ALL THINGS

Wikipedia
"Nataraja or Kooththan, The Lord (or King) of Dance, is a depiction of the god Shiva as the cosmic dancer who performs his divine dance to **destroy a weary universe** and make preparations for the god Brahma to start the process of creation"

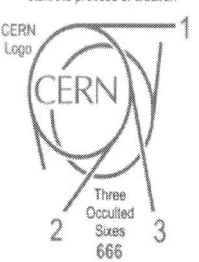

CERN Lab

CERN Logo

Three Occulted Sixes 666

1 2 3

Now let's get into the technological side of CERN so you can grasp how just how much power they can create and the elements that are used.

The CERN collider is composed of 9,600 super magnets, 100,000 times more powerful than the gravitational pull of Earth that fire protons around a circular track at tremendous speeds. A beam might rotate for up to 10 hours, travelling a distance of more than 10 billion kilometres, enough to make it to the far reaches of our Solar System and back again. Travelling just below the speed of light, a proton in the LHC will make 11,245 circuits every second. Yes, every second.

The magnet's coils, which are made up of 36 twisted 15mm strands, each strand comprised in turn of 6000-9000 single filaments, each filament possessing a diameter as small as 7 micrometres. The 27km length of the LHC demands some 7,600 km (4,100 miles) of cable, which amounts to about 270,000 km (145,000 miles) of strand, more than enough to circle the Earth six times at the Equator., yes, that's how much cable they have and you can imagine how much power they need to regulate it. I'll get to that later.

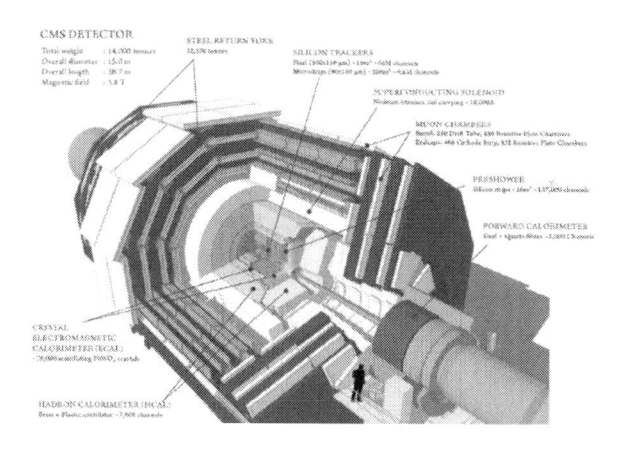

According to the CERN website, if the filaments were unravelled, they would *"stretch*

to the Sun and back five times with enough left over for a few trips to the Moon." Which is over 460 million miles. And I quite believe it.

The unbelievable hot temperatures it can reach is more than 100,000-times the temperature at the centre of the Sun. This has already been achieved at CERN, by accelerating and colliding together two beams of heavy ions. Considering the centre of the sun is 27 million degrees Fahrenheit- it's impressively hot.

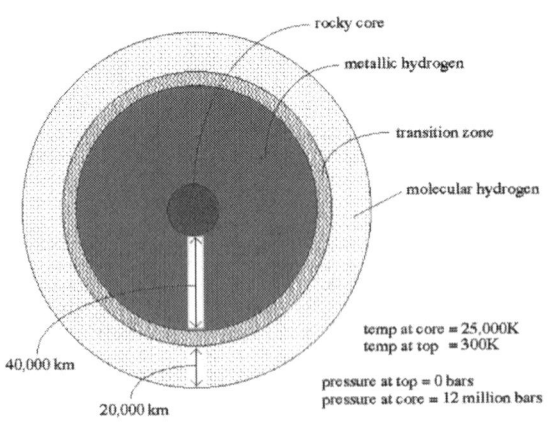

- rocky core
- metallic hydrogen
- transition zone
- molecular hydrogen

temp at core = 25,000K
temp at top = 300K

pressure at top = 0 bars
pressure at core = 12 million bars

40,000 km
20,000 km

CERN connects into this electromagnetic grid around us.

So, it's extremely powerful and people underestimate just how much energy it can produce and how much energy it needs to function.

To help them gain the energy they need-

HAARP/ionospheric heaters play a key role in the energy transformation in Earths ionosphere, take us back to 1985, Sacramento and the erection of a test antenna in the presence of Mr Bernard Eastland, the inventor of the technology and the man behind what would become known as HAARP - High Frequency Active Auroral Research Program.

What they are doing is transforming the atmosphere into an electrically charged plasma for various military uses, from weather manipulation to surveillance, down to the rearranging of our DNA.

Electromagnetism is all around you, they have the technology to manipulate it with HAARP as long as they have the right energy formats, they depend on plasma reactions that create big bursts of energy, then they tap into the energy waves for their own energy uses at CERN to create more power to achieve their goals.

SCIENTIFIC KNOWLEDGE ON HOW EMF EFFECTS THE PHYSICAL BODY

- Deteriorates melatonin in the body
- Destroys healthy blood cells
- Breaks apart DNA strands
- Changes firing rates in brain cells
- Leaks calcium ions in brain and cells
- Alters EEGs
- Most studies conducted at UCLA
- http://www.equilibra.uk.com/goafsbio.shtml Goldsworthy, Andrew (2007), The biological effects of weak electromagnetic fields

It is impossible to argue, with these findings, that EMF is safe, as the power companies have repeatedly stated.

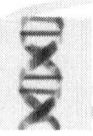

According to Wikipedia;

"The main instrument at HAARP is the Ionospheric Research Instrument (IRI). This is a high-power, high-frequency phased array radio transmitter with a set of 180 antennas, disposed in an array of 12x15

units that occupy a rectangle of about 30-40 acres (12-16 hectares). The IRI is used to temporarily energise a small portion of the ionosphere. The study of these disturbed volumes yields important information for understanding natural ionospheric processes. During active ionospheric research, the signal generated by the transmitter system is delivered to the antenna array and transmitted in an upward direction. At an altitude between 70 to 350 km (43 to 217 mi) (depending on operating frequency), the signal is partially absorbed in a small volume several tens of kilometres in diameter and a few meters thick over the IRI. The intensity of the HF signal in the ionosphere is less than $3 \mu W/cm^2$, tens of thousands of times less than the Sun's natural electromagnetic radiation reaching the Earth and hundreds of times less than even the normal random variations in intensity of the Sun's natural ultraviolet (UV) energy which creates the ionosphere. The small effects that are produced, however, can be observed with the sensitive scientific instruments installed at the HAARP facility, and these observations can provide information about the dynamics of plasmas and insight into the processes of solar-terrestrial interactions. Each antenna element consists of a crossed dipole that can be polarised for linear, ordinary mode (O-mode), or extraordinary mode (X-mode) transmission and reception. Each part of the two section crossed dipoles are individually fed from a specially designed, custom-built transmitter that operates at very low distortion levels. The Effective Radiated Power (ERP) of the IRI is limited by more than a factor of 10 at its lower operating frequencies. Much of this is due to higher antenna losses and a less efficient antenna pattern.

The IRI can transmit between 2.7 and 10 MHz, a frequency range that lies above the AM radio broadcast band and well below Citizens' Band frequency allocations. However, HAARP is licensed to transmit only in certain segments of this frequency range. When the IRI is transmitting, the bandwidth of the transmitted signal is 100 kHz or less. The IRI can transmit in continuous waves (CW) or in pulses as short as 10 microseconds (μs). CW transmission is generally used for ionospheric modification, while transmission in short pulses frequently repeated is used as a radar system. Researchers can run experiments that use both modes of transmission, first modifying the ionosphere for a predetermined amount of time, then measuring the decay of modification effects with pulsed transmissions.

There are other geophysical instruments for research located at the HAARP facility. Some of them are: -

A fluxgate magnetometer built by the University of Alaska Fairbanks Geophysical Institute, available to chart variations in the Earth's magnetic field. Rapid and sharp changes of the magnetic field may indicate a geomagnetic storm. A digisonde that can provide ionospheric profiles, allowing scientists to choose appropriate frequencies for IRI operation. The HAARP makes current and historic diagnosed information available online.

An induction magnetometer, provided by the University of Tokyo, that measures the changing geomagnetic field in the Ultra Low Frequency (ULF) range of 0-5 Hz.

The facility is powered by a set of five (5) 2500 kilowatt generators being driven by EMD 20-645-E4 diesel locomotive engines."

That's the "official" mainstream explanation, however; It isn't just conspiracy theorists who are concerned about HAARP. The European Union called the project a global concern and passed a resolution calling for more information on its health and environmental risks. Despite those concerns, officials at HAARP insist the project is nothing more sinister than a radio science research facility.

However, if you follow the documentation on HAARP weather control capabilities by Canada's CBC you'll begin to notice just how manipulating the ionosphere can alter atmosphere;

The temperature of the ionosphere has been raised by hundreds of degrees in these experiments.

A means and method are provided to cause interference with or even total disruption of communications over a very large portion of the Earth.

This invention could be employed to disrupt not only land-based communications, both civilian and military, but also airborne communications and sea communications. This would have significant military implications.

It is possible to take advantage of one or more such beams to carry out a communications network even though the rest of the world's communications are disrupted.

It can be used to an advantage for positive communication and eavesdropping purposes.

Exceedingly large amounts of power can be very efficiently produced and transmitted. This invention has a phenomenal variety of potential future developments.

Large regions of the atmosphere could be lifted to an unexpectedly high altitude so that missiles encounter unexpected and unplanned drag forces with resultant destruction or deflection.

Weather modification is possible by, for example, altering upper atmosphere wind patterns or altering solar absorption patterns by constructing one or more plumes of atmospheric particles which will act as a lens or focusing device. Ozone, nitrogen, etc. concentrations in the atmosphere could be artificially increased.

Electromagnetic pulse defences are also possible.

The Earth's magnetic field could be decreased or disrupted at appropriate altitudes to modify or eliminate the magnetic field.

With that being said, it is quite interesting to explore the patent description; it's is listed under the United States patent number: - 4686605 and was registered by Bernard J Eastlund who is an American physicist and one of the key figures at HAARP.

The patent description folds under questioning, considering they clearly state that they not altering the weather of any sort.

Here is what the patent states in the abstract: -

United States Patent 4,686,605
Eastlund August 11, 1987

Method and apparatus for altering a region in the earth's atmosphere, ionosphere, and/or magnetosphere

Abstract

A method and apparatus for altering at least one selected region which normally exists above the earth's surface. The region is excited by electron cyclotron resonance heating to thereby increase its charged particle density. In one embodiment, circularly polarized electromagnetic radiation is transmitted upward in a direction substantially parallel to and along a field line which extends through the region of plasma to be altered. The radiation is transmitted at a frequency which excites electron cyclotron resonance to heat and accelerate the charged particles. This increase in energy can cause ionization of neutral particles which are then absorbed as part of the region thereby increasing the charged particle density of the region.

Inventors: Eastlund; Bernard J. (Spring, TX)

The abstract alone clearly states that they are heating the ionosphere, altering plasma and increasing the charged particle density!? If you have studied particle physics and particle interaction, this would tell you that by increasing the charged particle density the ionosphere becomes super charged, meaning; the heating is what causes the super electrified plasma storms which is increasing worldwide. Not only is that worrying, if they can direct the energy into specific regions, they can steer the plasma waves which means they can steer low depressions such as; hurricanes, tropical storms etc to selective areas. The charged particles that cause these plasma reactions then have to release the energy which explodes causing an amazing spectacle: -

Gwen towers also play a vital role in CERNs goals, sixty-four elements in the ground modulate, with variation, the geomagnetic waves naturally coming from the ground. The Earth's natural 'brain rhythm' or 'heartbeat' (Schumann resonance) is balanced with these. These are the same minerals found in red blood corpuscles. There is a relation between the blood and geomagnetic waves. An imbalance between Schumann and geomagnetic waves disrupts these biorhythms. These natural geomagnetic waves are being replaced by artificially created low frequency

(LF) ground waves coming from GWEN Towers.

GWEN (Ground Wave Emergency Network) transmitters placed 200 miles apart across the USA allow specific frequencies to be tailored to the geomagnetic-field strength in each area, allowing the magnetic field to be altered. They operate in the LF range, with transmissions between LF 150 and 175 KHz. They also emit waves from the upper VHF to the lower UHF range of 225 - 400 MHz. The LF signals travel by waves that hug the ground rather than radiating into the atmosphere. A GWEN station transmits in a 360-degree circle up to 300 miles, the signal dropping off sharply with distance. The entire GWEN system consists of, (depending on source of data), from 58 to an intended 300 transmitters spread across the USA, each with a tower 299-500 ft high. 300 ft copper wires in spoke-like fashion fan out from the base of the system underground, interacting with the Earth, like a thin shelled conductor, radiating radio wave energy for very long distances through the ground. In the UK or other smaller countries, the Gwen towers are situated closer together and range between 30ft-150ft, there is much less ground mass to travel so they don't need to be as high therefore it's important for them to be closer together for them to be interconnected through a constant flow of low frequencies.

The United States is bathed in this magnetic field which can rise from the ground up to 500 ft, but goes down into basements, so everyone can be affected and mind-controlled. The entire artificial ground-wave spreads out over the whole of the USA like a web. It is easier to mind-control and hypnotise people who are bathed in an artificial electromagnetic-wave. Same goes for all countries now as the projects are near completion worldwide.

GWEN transmitters have many different functions including: -

1. controlling the weather.

2. mind control.

3. behaviour and mood control.

4. sending synthetic-telepathy as infrasound to victims with US government mind-control implants.

5. **Allows CERN to interact with the frequency emitted.**

GWEN works in conjunction with HAARP and the Russian Woodpecker transmitter: -

which is similar to HAARP. The Russians openly market a small version of their weather-engineering system called Elate, which can fine-tune weather patterns over a 200-mile area and have the same range as the GWEN unit. An Elate system operates at Moscow airport. The GWEN towers shoot enormous bursts of energy into the atmosphere in conjunction with HAARP. The website http:-//www.cuttingedge.org wrote to expose of how the major floods of the Mid-West USA occurred in 1993. All connects to CERN and the coming pole shift.

Basically, the goal is that they need the overall 'frequency' of each victim to function at a specific rate below the threshold of awareness to allow the new dimension to occur.

Vaccine Implants are now smaller than a hair's width and are injected with vaccine and flu shots.

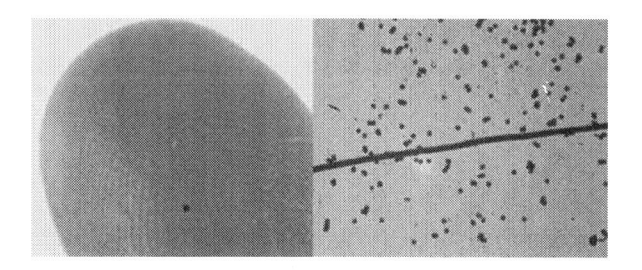

Millions have had this done unknowingly. These 'biochips' circulate in the bloodstream and lodge in the brain, enabling the victims to hear 'voices' via the implant. There are many kinds of implants now and 1 in 40 are victims from 'alien abduction' statistics, though 1 in 20 has also been gauged. The fake alien abduction event, revealed to be actually the work of US military personnel using technology to make hologram spaceships outside, virtual reality scenarios of going onto a spaceship with humans in costumes, has been astutely perceived i.e. 'project blue beam'. The 'alien abduction' scenario has been useful to stop any further investigation or accountability of government authorities by poor victims who would face mockery and appear silly.

Chemtrails also play a role for CERN. turning the sky into a battery, or an antenna.

The metal particulates, and the Nano-tech contained within, are being inhaled by us and gradually make you more susceptible to the frequency manipulators, like Gwen towers, which tap into your energy which is just a certain frequency to put you in a more lower state, make you conform to the norm of what the elite say/do, more control, nanobots can be programmed to alter your DNA... just like they do in labs. 5G will be rolled out to increase the manipulation of these frequencies.

Chemtrails and the metal particulates and other filth contained within are an essential ingredient to all of this. The metals, barium and aluminium, are required to turn the atmosphere into an ionised plasma, just what is required for all of the above to be possible. They are also used to obscure the view of the incoming planetary bodies.

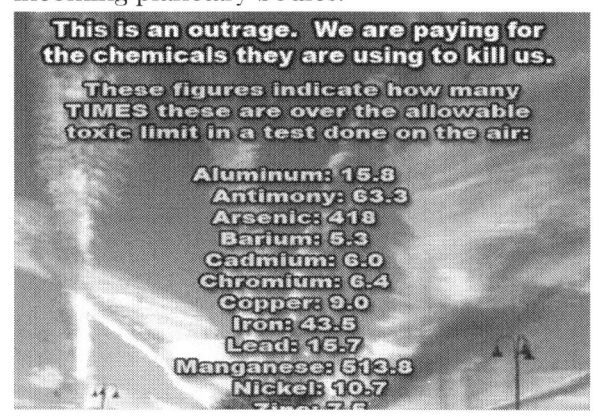

> This is an outrage. We are paying for the chemicals they are using to kill us.
> These figures indicate how many TIMES these are over the allowable toxic limit in a test done on the air:
> Aluminum: 15.8
> Antimony: 63.3
> Arsenic: 418
> Barium: 5.3
> Cadmium: 6.0
> Chromium: 6.4
> Copper: 9.0
> Iron: 43.5
> Lead: 15.7
> Manganese: 513.8
> Nickel: 10.7

'Lockheed Martin' are the ones behind the design of this systems and on the face of it seems pretty harmless. Here's what Lockheed have to say about the 'Space Fence' (one of the operations, black op funded) on their own site-

"Lockheed Martin is currently developing its technology solution for Space Fence, a program that will revamp the way the U.S. Air Force identifies and tracks objects in space. Space Fence will use S-band ground-based radars to provide the Air Force with uncured detection, tracking and accurate measurement of space objects, primarily in low-Earth orbit. The geographic separation and the higher wave frequency of the new Space Fence radars will allow for the detection of much smaller micro-satellites and debris than current systems. Additionally, Lockheed Martin's Space Fence design will significantly improve the timeliness with which operators can detect space events which could present potential threats to GPS satellites or the International Space Station. Space Fence will replace the existing Air Force Space Surveillance System, or VHF Fence, which has been in service since the early 1960s. The new system's initial operational capability is scheduled for 2018.

With more than 400 operational S-band arrays deployed worldwide, Lockheed Martin is a leader in S-band radar development, production, operation and sustainment. The Lockheed Martin-led team, which includes General Dynamics, AT&T and AMEC, has decades of collective experience in space-related programs including sensors, mission-processing, cataloguing, orbital mechanics, net-centric communications and facilities."

Sounds harmless right?

Wrong.

The Space Fence, HAARP, CERN, wind turbines, fracking, smart meters, Gwen towers and smartphones are just some parts of the electromagnetic prison being formed invisibly all around us and are being unwillingly used by us the consumers.

They use fluoride to attack your pineal gland also, this will give you make you become depressed/sad/tired and less bothered about the world events taking place which allows the elite to operate easier, that's why they put fluoride in your tap water, along with lead, aluminium and other acidic substances, all to make you ill. Then you turn to 'big pharma' for prescription drugs which line the pockets of the elite.

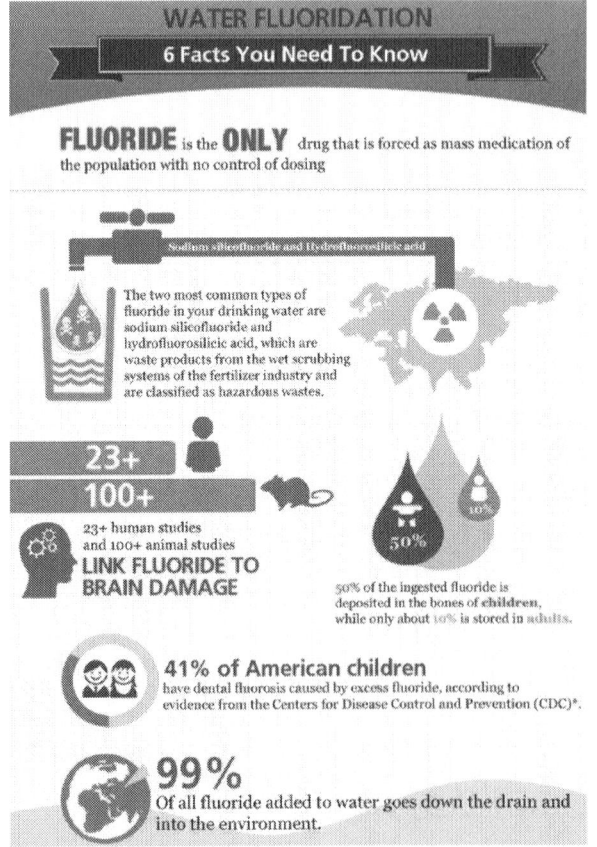

WATER FLUORIDATION
6 Facts You Need To Know

FLUORIDE is the **ONLY** drug that is forced as mass medication of the population with no control of dosing

Sodium silicofluoride and Hydrofluorosilicic acid

The two most common types of fluoride in your drinking water are sodium silicofluoride and hydrofluorosilicic acid, which are waste products from the wet scrubbing systems of the fertilizer industry and are classified as hazardous wastes.

23+
100+

23+ human studies and 100+ animal studies
LINK FLUORIDE TO BRAIN DAMAGE

50% of the ingested fluoride is deposited in the bones of **children**, while only about 10% is stored in adults.

41% of American children have dental fluorosis caused by excess fluoride, according to evidence from the Centers for Disease Control and Prevention (CDC)*.

99%
Of all fluoride added to water goes down the drain and into the environment.

It's one big game to them.

Well they have made Earth a giant lab in in preparation for what's coming.

Our natural environment is being changed into an artificial construct, swimming in electromagnetic signals, with all of us slowly being integrated into this matrix forming around us.

You must understand the negative forces that they work for and worship. If you don't believe in the spiritual world then you may as well stop reading this now because nothing from here on will make sense to you.

The universe is full of different dimensions, different vibrations, different frequencies, different sounds. The one you are able to see is completely synchronised to your perception, our physical realm, that's our dimension.

You have higher dimensions, higher frequencies, different wavelengths, strings of energy that you can surround yourself in by being of kind nature, compassionate, loving, caring and being truthful. Those things are the basis of having a "good vibe" which others will feel/sense as the energy emits from you thus attracting the positive vibrations.

Then you have the lower form of dimensions, the lower frequencies, lower wavelengths, the strings of energy that most do not want to surround themselves in, these dimensions are where the evil live, the dark forces of nature, the demonic entities that feed off the energy you emit. When you get a "bad vibe" about a place or a person, that's your energies picking up on something, listen to it.

Both of these dimensions are all around you 24/7 waiting to attach themselves to the surrounding strings of energy that is emitted around the energy you emit.

This is why the elite make sure there is false flags to create: -

panic/fear/anger/confusion/sadness because these are the emotions that put you in lower state of consciousness which means they can tap into that consciousness through the lower frequency...so you see?

Most of the bombings/mass murders in schools etc are all set up for this.

Most people don't understand when they are saying it's a "false flag";

For example – the Manchester terrorist attack that occurred a music concert hosted by Arianna Grande in 2017;

To call a 'situation' a false flag does not mean that it did not occur; people are not doubting a bomb went off and that people were killed and injured as a result. That is not what's being called into question. When people say something is a false flag it means they're doubting who is/was behind the attack/scandal as it's being presented by the mainstream media.

In this particular instance the mainstream media is covering the story in Manchester with an unmissable "TERRORIST ATTACK" bolded and highlighted as they're presenting the story to us. Due to being conditioned by multiple false flags throughout history people associate scary bolded "TERRORIST ATTACK" with outside terrorism and automatically leap to conclusions with the aid of the media that these attacks were carried out by 'foreign' terrorists.

A few days after we will begin to see interviews on TV with government officials discussing/reassuring our safety as though we had reason to be worried, which further propels the assumption that it WAS a terrorist attack. Speculation becomes "fact" as the public is further persuaded that the claims made by mainstream media just minutes after the attack occurred are actually true. All without tangible evidence, simply just by media manipulation. These systematic events are used to condition us.

By calling this attack a "false flag" means people are doubting the SOURCE of the terror: - which essentially is doubting what the mainstream media is presenting to the public.

"False flag operations are covert operations conducted by governments, corporations, or other organisations, which are designed to deceive the public in such a way that the operations appear as if they are being carried out by other entities. The name is derived from the military concept of flying false colours; that is, flying the flag of a country other than one's own."

So, to reiterate: - people calling an incident a "false flag" does not mean they doubt an attack/scandal occurred or that people were injured or killed.

What they doubt is the "who" as it's being portrayed to the public.

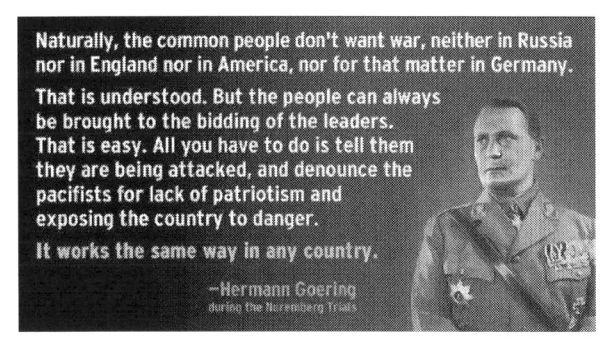

> Naturally, the common people don't want war, neither in Russia nor in England nor in America, nor for that matter in Germany.
>
> That is understood. But the people can always be brought to the bidding of the leaders. That is easy. All you have to do is tell them they are being attacked, and denounce the pacifists for lack of patriotism and exposing the country to danger.
>
> It works the same way in any country.
>
> —Hermann Goering
> during the Nuremberg Trials

The elite are doing everything in their power to change our frequency and Earths frequency to bring forth this dimension into the physical realm which is why they all worship the same Gods, which are all just the same one God.

Yes, the beast, Satan, baphomet, moloch, nimrod, lucifer etc .... he comes in many disguises remember, they are all as one, the spirit of evil. The evil that comes through won't be a horned beast, it will be like us.

This is why they say things like this-

Sergio Bertolucci, former Director for Research and Scientific Computing of the facility- ''we will be able to open dimensional doors, a very tiny lapse of time," mere fractions of a second. However, that may be just enough time "to peer into this open door, either by getting something out of it or sending something into it."

> **Director of Research**
>
> "Something may come through' dimensional 'doors' at LHC". And "Out of this door might come something, or we might send something through it." -Sergio Bertolucci, Director for Research and Scientific Computing at CERN.

They say this because they have already done it, opened worm holes to the other dimension they are seeking, the demonic realm.

Gordie rose is a key player at CERN, he is the driving force behind the D-Wave "interdimensional" quantum computer.

GEORDIE ROSE, THE MAN BEHIND THE QUANTUM MASK
ANTHONY PATCH - THE KEV BAKER SHOW, EP#049

The D-Wave is an Adiabatic Quantum Computer (AQC) that is described as an "alter to an alien God" That's not my words, they belong to the main man at D-Wave, Mr Geordie Rose. It's capable of accessing different dimensions on a quantum level, like a fast track to contact other beings and even states they ''they are summoning'' entities that do not care about the existence of humans.

They don't just say these things for no reason, they are trying to play it down with slight humour knowing that people will unwillingly accept it because they make it sound so normal.

Even the name D-WAVE hides the symbolic meaning-

D:·WaVe
The Quantum Computing Company™

Compute this

DeMeN :·
The Quantum Computing Company™

Coincidence? No such thing when you know exactly how the occult work.

Please watch the video link provided to here, all what Geordie rose says in a seminar to school graduates, yes, he is trying to enlist them and this video gives a very good explanation of how they work- https://youtu.be/iJQkwnkNSPc

Now we get to the part where they have to show you the CERN symbolism through television adverts/films/tv shows.

In this advert, you can view it here:- https://youtu.be/skJUuY-VKxo

It shows a car going through a portal into another dimension. But when you see all the other symbolism, you will always notice the real meaning behind the mainstream advert, I'll add some still shots so you can understand better before watching the video in your own time-

Here you will see a 'Peugeot' car, the logo for Peugeot is a lion which represents the 'beast': -

PEUGEOT

The portal in the advert represents CERN, so the beast is coming through a quantum portal from a strange computer room into the real world: -

Then we see the big circular machine begin to turn on in the quantum form of dimensional states whilst the car is primed ready to go through the portal: -

Then we see the car drive through the quantum portal into another dimension: -

After the 'beast' goes through the 'portal' the car then comes out into our world: -

Not only do they come into our world but they also ironically enter through the 'barren land'- (*Jeremiah 2: -6*)

Then as they are driving over the bridge (bridge of lucifer) as a whale jumps over them as if it was 'free' and at the same time shows the whales 'belly' as it jumps over.

This represents the 'belly of the beast' being set 'free' into the 'physical realm' and the humans are acting all happy. And the narrator even says at the end "enter a new dimension".

This is how they work, hidden in plain sight. To the untrained eye you would think it's just an advert.

Same goes for the Audi advert: - https:-//youtu.be/QnMxcM7Gbjo

It's called 'birth'

I'll add some still shots again so it's easier to understand-

the beast (roaring car) coming through the dimensional door birthing the beast: -

Then the cracking of the veil, the abyss...coming into the physical realm: -

Coincidence? No such thing.

Here's a video of how CERN has been shown on television for years, 'RoundSaturnsEye' YouTube channel has been exposing these for years, if you are religious or not, I'd suggest watching them as he does give good explanations of how they show you things in plain sight- https:-//youtu.be/YcQWtnoz2JA

Here's another, the illuminati are very satanic, rituals are needed to gain the negative frequencies they need. They are the ones that are controlling this prison planet. https:-//youtu.be/lb8_VWOHgy8

CERN symbolism everywhere. https:-//youtu.be/1dI0gdqsUhI

The opening of the tunnel at CERN as you can see, all represents the God they serve, a ritual and here it's the exact same concept, the zombies coming out of the abyss, the demonic 'entities' coming through the veil: -

After they come out of the abyss, they all start parading around horned beasts: -

Not long after, they begin to bow down to a fallen angel, this represents the God they serve, the satanic allegiance: -

As they come out of the tunnel, they all go forward to a screen and pay their respects to a horned beast that is being portrayed in front of them whilst the worldly figures watch from the audience clapping: -

So, as you can see, these are much more than coincidences.

The cube of Saturn represents the matrix (saturnalia) pagan. They have the black cubs around the world to show their world domination. https:-//youtu.be/GL0_vdIAGL4

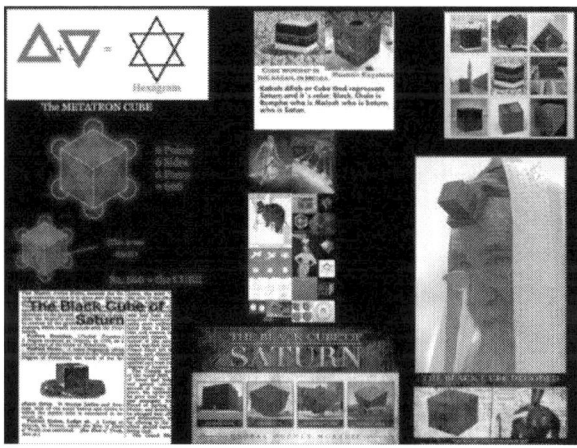

Same again here, dancing through the matrix, the cosmic dance, ritual, in the 'barren land' https:-//youtu.be/Cllqr1nmdYk :-

Google- CERN symmetry dance, very ritualistic.

Even celebrities have to pay their respects with symbolism when it comes to CERN, to remain rich and famous: -

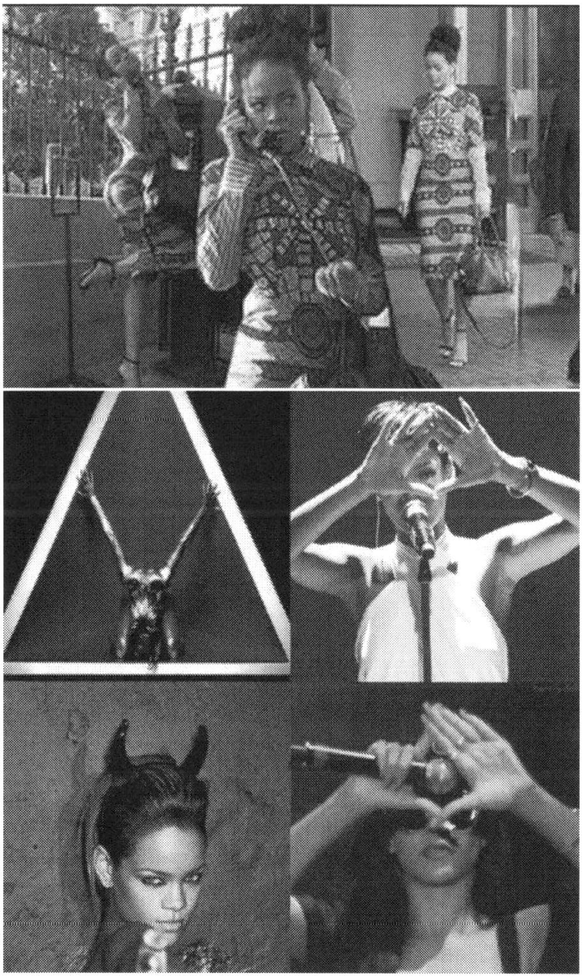

I could add hundreds of videos here but by now, if you've watched the above, you'll catch the gist of what's really going on and how they are manipulating frequencies to bring hell on Earth, literally.

What's the biggest tool of the underworld?

Science.

What does this have to do with the pole shift??

First you need to understand what causes the pole shift.

Every ancient religion/scripture/prophecy/book/tablets/carving/painting all depict what they experienced and showed us what they saw in the skies, how the water came to shore, how they had to run to the mountains: -

SPIRAL
GRAB YOUR FAMILY AND RUN
TO WHERE THE GOATS ARE

SPIRAL   MEN
         GOATS

How they saw green/purple men in the sky (plasma discharges): -

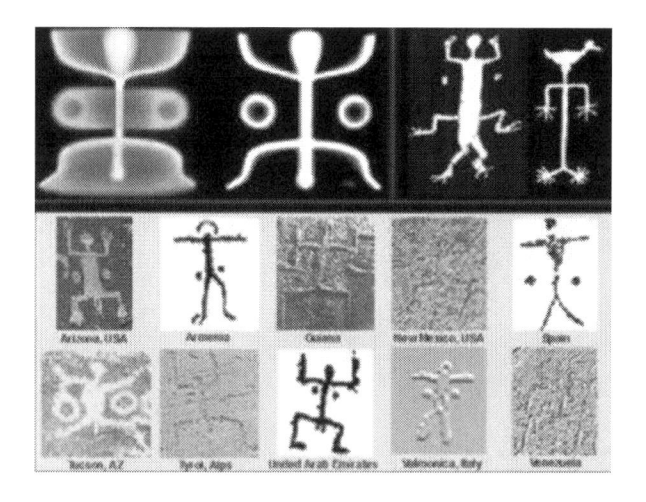

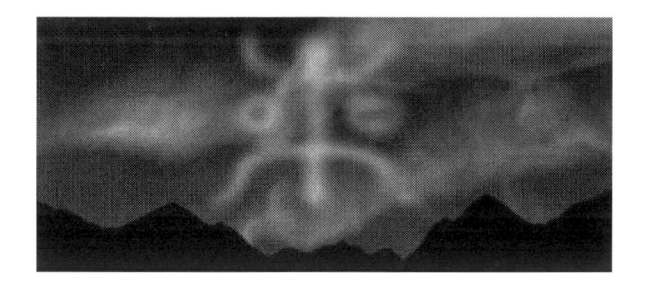

How the clouds rolled back, how the
Earthquakes occurred causing destruction
after seeing spirals in the skies, from different
accounts from all over the globe with no form

of contacting each other yet all talk of the
same things and depicted them in their
drawings/carvings: -

LOCATIONS OF SPIRAL PETROGLYPHS

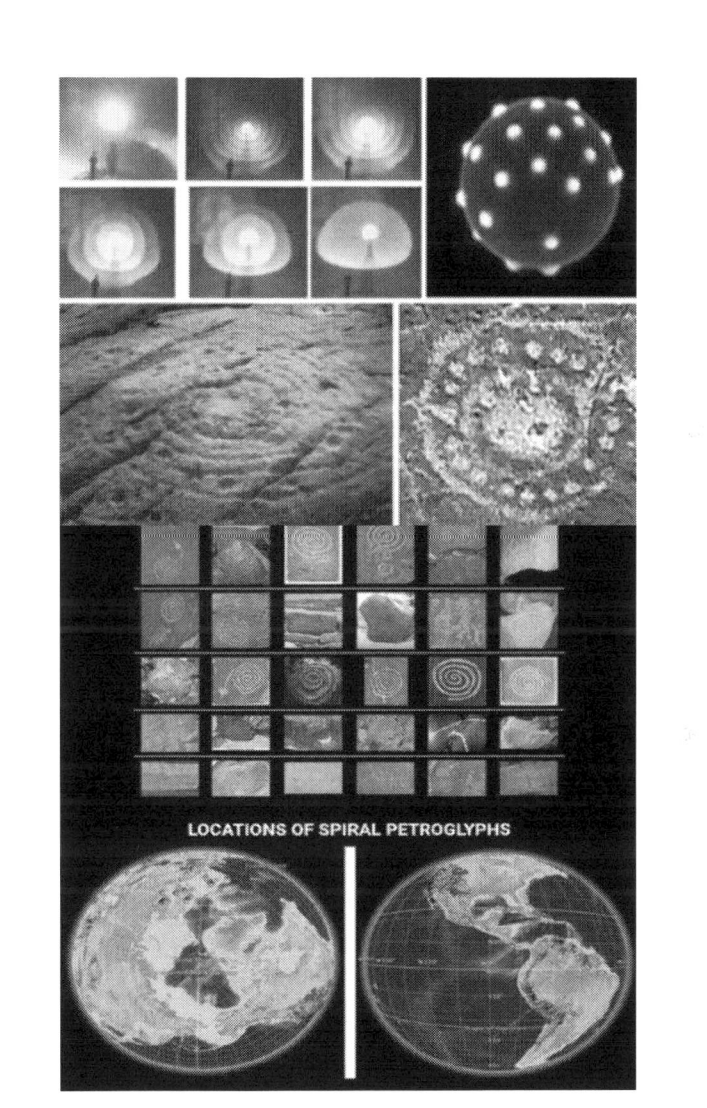

How the volcanoes erupted, how the fish of the sea died, how the land animals perished, how mountains were moved, how deserts became oceans and oceans become desserts, how the birds fell out of the sky etc which refers to the bible -

"Because of this the land dries up, and all who live in it waste away, the beasts of the field, the birds in the sky and the fish in the sea are swept away." Hosea 4: -3

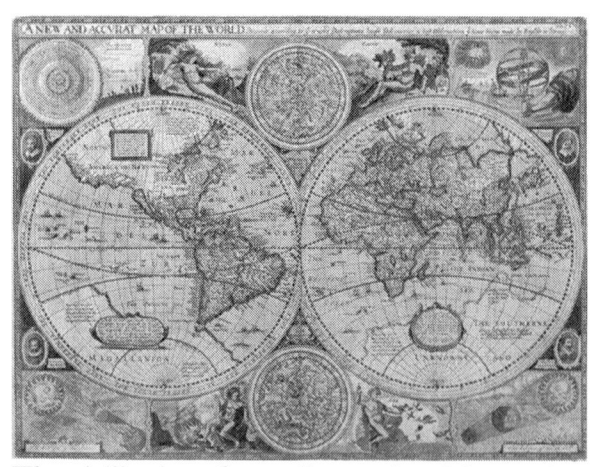

The civilisations from all over the globe spoke of the exact same events through the same years even though they had no form of contacting the people around the world? then thousands of years apart the same story has been told from different parts of the world also.

That's pretty compelling evidence in itself but it doesn't stop there.

There are cities that have been found under the oceans that was covered with water suddenly and there has been big boats found in mountains- that itself speaks volumes.

But what causes it?

All ancient civilisations carved/painted more planets in our solar system than we are taught, 'nibiru' is the 'planet of the crossing' that is spoken of extensively in the ancient Sumerian teachings and is part of the 'nemesis system' as already stated.

sol   nibiru   marduk

Nemesis is the central star mass and is a brown dwarf star, very dense, helium, lithium, iron oxide. The electromagnetic properties of a brown dwarf are very strong, the system has a very long elliptical orbit around our sun, every 3650(ish) years this system comes back into our solar system and creates an immense amount of galactic energy through our entire solar system.

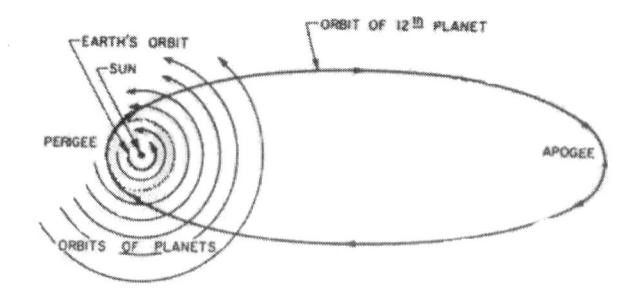

When you watch data, you can connect the dots quite easily.

The system has to come back through our Kuiper belt (asteroid belt) on its way to reach its perihelion around the sun, 20 years ago, that's exactly what it done and that's why every year we have thousands more fireball/near Earth asteroids events than the previous years and the previous years before that, the magnetic power of the system grabs tons of debris as it passes it and the system knocked tons of debris towards us as it came through. Notice the increase in events: -

American Meteor Society

Events

All countries | 2002

All types ▼ | All number of reports

All Event

Events found: 5 in 2002

American Meteor Society

Events

All countries | 2003

All types ▾ | All number of reports

All Event

Events found: 8 in 2003

American Meteor Society

Events

All countries | 2004

All types ▾ | All number of reports

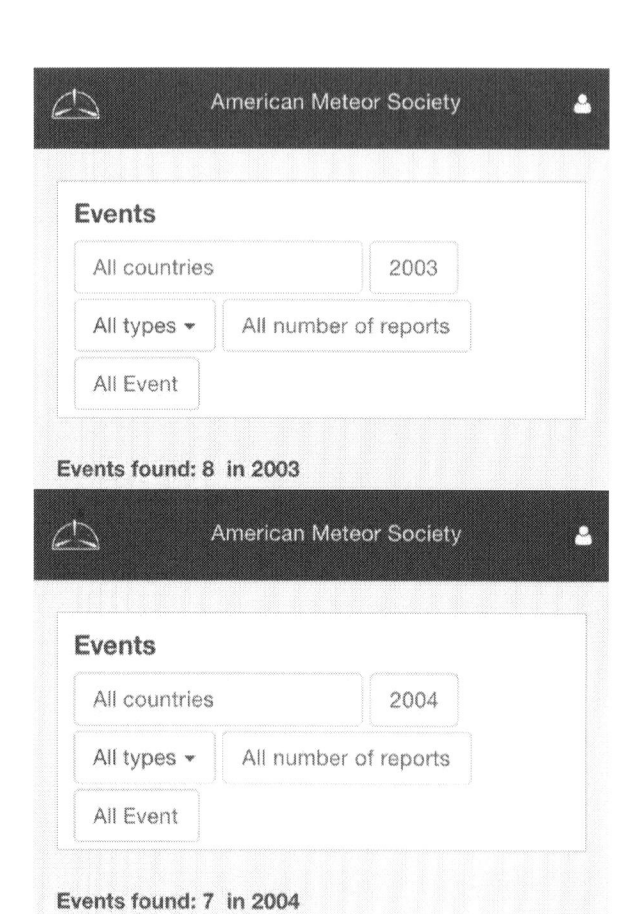

All Event

Events found: 7 in 2004

American Meteor Society

Events

| All countries | 2005 |

All types ▾ | All number of reports

All Event

Events found: 459 in 2005   Page 1 / 10

American Meteor Society

Events

| All countries | 2006 |

All types ▾ | All number of reports

All Event

Events found: 495 in 2006   Page 1 / 10

American Meteor Society

Events

All countries | 2007

All types ▾ | All number of reports

All Event

Events found: 569 in 2007   Page 1 / 12

American Meteor Society

Events

All countries | 2008

All types ▾ | All number of reports

All Event

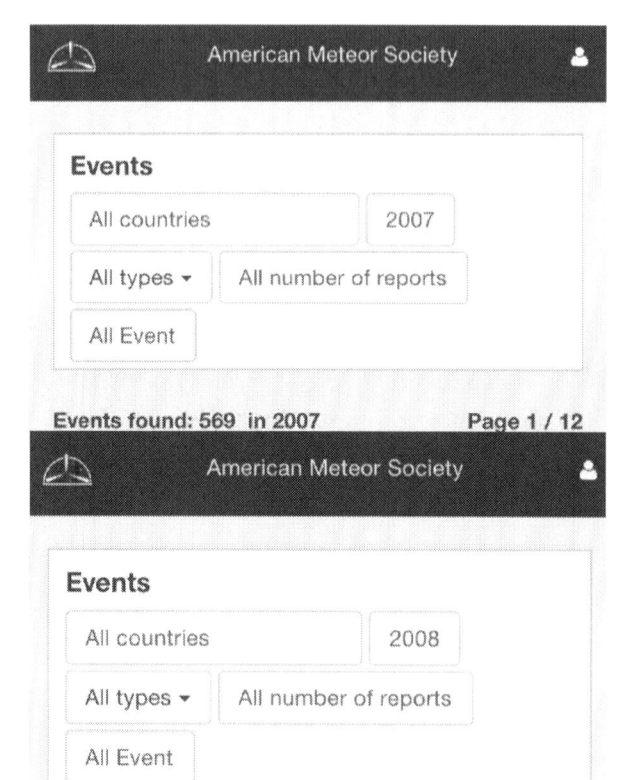

Events found: 713 in 2008   Page 1 / 15

American Meteor Society

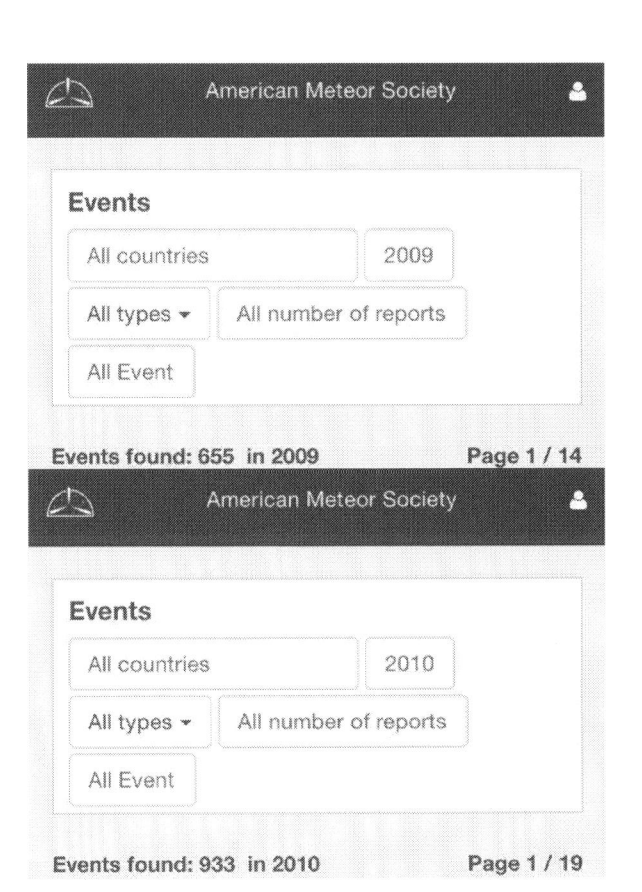

Events

All countries | 2009

All types ▾ | All number of reports

All Event

Events found: 655 in 2009 — Page 1 / 14

American Meteor Society

Events

All countries | 2010

All types ▾ | All number of reports

All Event

Events found: 933 in 2010 — Page 1 / 19

American Meteor Society

Events

All countries | 2011

All types ▾ | All number of reports

All Event

Events found: 1636 in 2011 | **Page 1 / 33**

American Meteor Society

Events

All countries | 2012

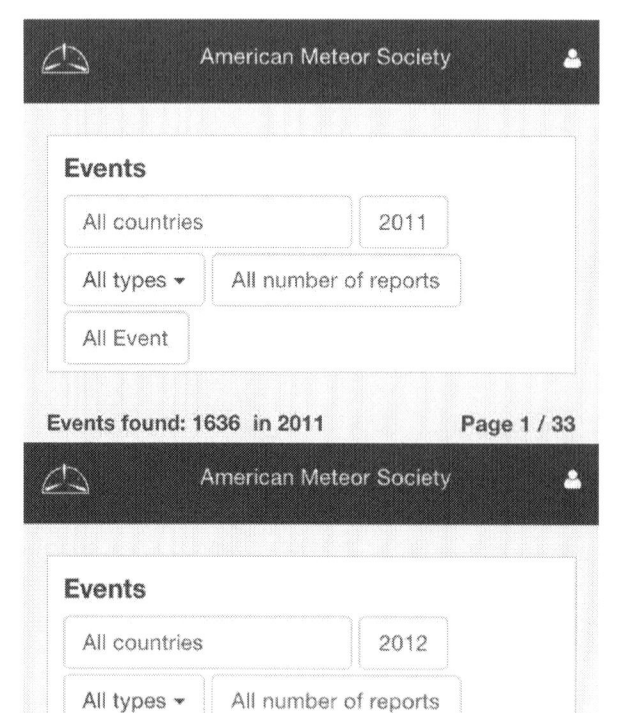

All types ▾ | All number of reports

All Event

Events found: 2162 in 2012 | **Page 1 / 44**

American Meteor Society

Events

All countries | 2013

All types ▾ | All number of reports

All Event

Events found: 3578 in 2013   **Page 1 / 72**

American Meteor Society

Events

All countries | 2014

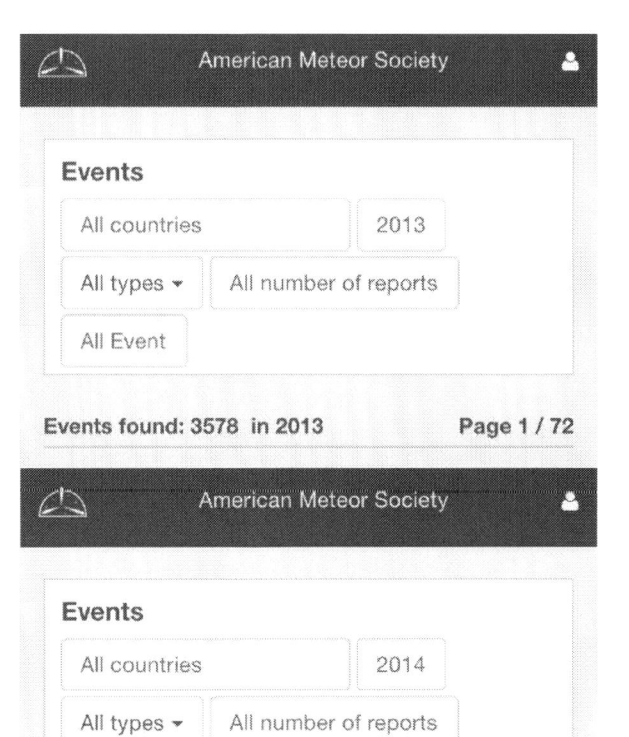

All types ▾ | All number of reports

All Event

Events found: 3774 in 2014   **Page 1 / 76**

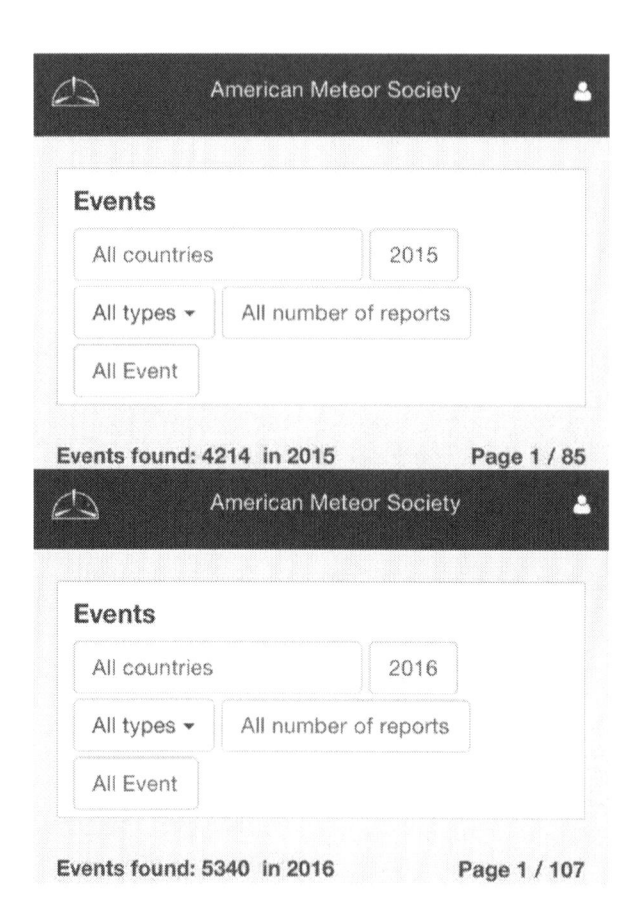

So, as you can see, the events have become progressively risen as the years go by meaning; the debris field becomes closer to Earths orbital path thus meaning the system gets closer every year.

Some people may state that the satellite detection systems have been upgraded through the years but it's still the exact same satellites with the exact same technologies.

Remember the NASA live announcement about finding a solar system on the edge of ours last year? Well this is how they work, truth mixed with disinformation. They said the system has a brown dwarf star as the central star mass with 7 orbiting planets and they called it the 'Trappist 1' system, which is a Catholic religious order so you know who's behind it (illuminati) as always.

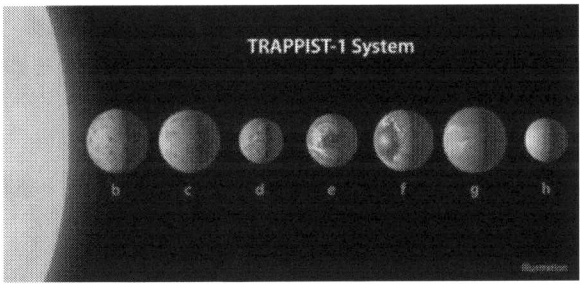

So, they are describing the exact same system we have spoken of for years. And spoiler alert, it's not 39 lightyears away, it's right in our back yard.

The elite have known about this for a very, very long time but the 1950s was where some of the government agencies caught hold of what was happening and word spread, it made papers but was swiftly stopped from ever being published again due to the amount of panic it was causing.

Planet X Delays Comet's Arrival

LIVERMORE, Calif. AP — "Intolerable errors" in the predicted timetable of Halley's Comet have led a University of California scientific team to believe a 10th planet may be circling the sun beyond Pluto — outermost known planet in the solar system.

Three computer scientists at the University's Lawrence Livermore Laboratory said Friday their prediction of the planet's existence is based on mathematical calculations related to the orbit of the mysterious Comet.

The team, led by Joseph L. Brady, named the proposed body "Planet X." According to the scientists, the planet would be 300 times more massive than earth and about six billion miles from the sun — far beyond the orbit of Pluto. The earth is 93 million miles from the sun.

The planet would take 512 years to make a single revolution around the sun, and its orbit would be sharply tilted other nine planets revolve, the scientists said.

Brady said he came up with the "Planet X" theory after studying unexplained orbital deviations of Halley's Comet. He said he concluded the deviations could be caused by the gravitational action of "Planet X."

The scientist said past predictions of the arrival of Halley's Comet near earth have repeatedly been wrong by several days.

"Errors like those are intolerable and they demanded an explanation," Brady said. "They couldn't be satisfactorily explained by the turmoil in the gases of the comet's tail as it approached the sun, but they fit precisely into a gravitational picture of the solar system that

(Continued On Page Two)

10th Planet A Possibility

LIVERMORE, Calif. (AP) — The existence of a 10th planet in the earth's solar system was suggested Friday by scientists at the University of California's Lawrence Livermore Laboratory.

The planet, the outermost in the solar system, never has been seen. The prediction it exists is based on new and sophisticated mathematical calculations at the laboratory.

The proposed body—dubbed "Planet X" by scientists—would be three times as large as Saturn and twice as far as Neptune from the sun.

Earth, the third nearest to the sun of the nine known planets, is 80 times smaller than Saturn and nearly three billion miles from Neptune.

The calculations which led to Planet X evolved from studies of Halley's Comet, whose orbit contains mysterious deviations and whose appearance to earth can never be predicted with accuracy.

The calculations were made by a team of three scientists at the Lawrence Livermore Laboratory. Joseph L. Brady, a supervisor in numerical techniques wrote up the team's finding in next Monday's edition of the Journal of the Astronomical Society of the Pacific.

Brady, an acknowledged authority on Halley's Comet, said the prediction of new planets based on mathematical calculations was not new. Neptune's location was predicted in 1846 in a similar way.

To make his predictions, Brady used information from previous observations of Halley's Comet, which has been reported since before the birth of Christ. With the laboratory's enormous computer system he worked out the planet's pro

"The proposed planet cated in the densely pop Milky Way where even a area encompasses thousan stars," Brady said, "ma which are brighter than w pect this planet to be."

"If it exists, it will b tremely difficult to find, added.

Brady said his method o culating the location and s the planet was based on a bitrary mathematical which would account for tions in the last four ap ances of Halley's Comet then translated that math tical term into the pro planet's mass and location

Subsequent calculations termined that existence o proposed planet would ex variations in the orbits o other known comets and not contradict what is kno the orbits of the other plan

The proposed planet take about 512 years to the sun and probably wou bit in an opposite directio the other planets, Brady a

Astronomers made ar depth planet search bet 1930 and 1936, but calcula show their search was jus side the area where the would be located, Brady s

Quincy Water Rated High In Bacteria Conte

BOSTON (UPI) — The Environmental Protection cy has banned the use o city of Quincy's water s from use on interstate car on grounds it "has fail meet the bacteriological re ments" set by federal stand it was announced Friday.

"Although we have ha indications of any sicknes tributed directly to the dri of city water," said John McGlennon, regional admin tor of the U.S. Environm Protection Agency, "we are cerned at the high bac content and have urged th to take immediate steps t rect the situation."

and forestry committee was told Thursday.

J. S. Tener, director general of the environment department's Canadian wildlife service, said there are between 6,000 and 10,000 polar bears in Canada and their population is increasing, particularly in the James Bay area.

trolled over-hunting by those countries.

In the Canadian north hunting from snowmobiles and aircraft was not allowed; only the "primitive hunting experience" by dog sled was licensed.

He was also optimistic about the immediate future of duck and geese populations.

Baker paroled

WASHINGTON (AP) — Bobby Baker, one-time protege of President Lyndon B. Johnson, was granted parole Thursday from a one-to-three-year sentence he currently is serving for attempted tax evasion and related charges.

The 43-year-old Baker was denied parole last December but the United States parole board announced Thursday he will be freed from the Allenwood, Pa., federal prison camp on June 1.

He began serving his sentence Jan. 14, 1971.

Baker, one-time Senate page boy who became secretary to the Senate Democratic majority, was convicted in U.S. district court in Washington in 1967 on charges of attempted tax evasion, grand larceny, transportation of stolen money, fraud and conspiracy.

Crowds dispersed

BUENOS AIRES (Reuter) — Police firing tear-gas grenades Friday night dispersed about 1,500 persons who tried to hold a banned "hunger march" in protest against the Argentine military government's economic policies.

Police and troops outnumbered the marchers four to one.

Small groups stoned police and some threw gasoline bombs and tried to build barricades. Police said they arrested 273 persons.

Two bombs exploded near the Casa Rosada (Pink House) where President Alejandro Lanusse has his offices. This was the goal of the marchers, who had a petition for the president.

A child received serious injuries to a hand and a building was damaged, eyewitnesses said.

About 5,000 police and 1,500 troops sealed off the central business and entertainment district of the city. The police were backed up by water-cannon and armored cars.

10th planet suggested

LIVERMORE, Calif. (AP) — The existence of a 10th planet in the earth's solar system was suggested Friday by scientists at the University of California's Lawrence Livermore Laboratory.

The planet, the outermost in the solar system, never has been seen, and the supposition that it exists is based on new and sophisticated mathematical calculations at the laboratory.

The proposed body—dubbed "Planet X" by scientists—would be three times as large as Saturn and twice as far as Neptune from the sun.

Earth, the third nearest to the sun of the nine known planets, is 80 times smaller than Saturn and nearly three billion miles from Neptune.

The calculations concerning Planet X evolved from the studies of Halley's Comet. The comet's orbit contains mysterious deviations and its appearance to earth has never been predicted with accuracy

9
many people in, mom. That cake
hen you last saw it."

If woman are used as bus drivers
they never will be able to get men
to go to the back of the bus.

Merry-Go-Round
w Pearson

had been able to hold their lines
together for evacuation purposes.
"It looks like we will have to
evacuate and I think the navy can
handle its end of the job," Sherman
said.
He added, however, that there
might be "losses" if the navy had
to contend with Russian attack
planes and submarines.
"But even if that happens we'll
still get the job done," the admiral predicted.

Lagging Airplane Production

Sherman's realistic report had an
electrifying effect on the committee and its salty chairman, Representative Carl Vinson of Georgia.
Vinson announced that he wouldn't
stand for any more "business as
usual" in the war production program.
The Georgian spoke his piece
when William J. McNeil, assistant
secretary of defense, advised the
committee behind closed doors that
aircraft production wasn't moving
too fast because of delays in getting airplane engines.
"Plants producing engines are on
an eight-hour work day and at this
rate it will be 18 months before
warplane production will be at a
peak," McNeil reported.
"Well, those plants ought to be
working on a 24-hour basis," shot
back Vinson. "We've got to get
the job done now—not 18 months
from now. We won't get it done
with men working only eight hours
a day. Money is not the object
now. Our liberty and the freedom
of the world is at stake."

Barren-Brained Senators

Colorado's GOP Senator Eugene
Millikin, whose head is as smooth
as a Colorado boulder, gave his
opinion the other day of senators
who try to conceal their baldness.
Millikin took the floor in self-
defense at a closed-door Republican caucus, after Maine's Senator
Owen Brewster made a crack about
bald-headed old-timers. Mischievously Millikin accused Brewster of
trying to cover his bald head with
"slicked overs," or strands of strategically combed hair.
"But the greatest deceptionist is
Bob Taft," grinned Millikin with a
glance at Senator Taft's thinly
camouflaged head.

blic Opinion
rean Decisions

D LAWRENCE

American public opinion has won
ement. There is to be no surrender
ighting will go on. Evacuation of
cur only in those places where the
ing number of troops.

ys.
are last several days have brought

Planet Pluto Almost Defies Measurements

By J. HUGH PRUETT
University of Oregon

Scientific exhilaration seized
both professional astronomers and
the interested public when on
March 13, 1930, the newspaper
headlines proclaimed the finding
by Clyde Tombaugh of the Lowell
observatory at Flagstaff, Ariz., of
a faint, starlike object in the constellation Gemini.
This was announced as another
planet traveling in an orbit far
more distant from the sun than
that of Neptune. Since its discovery, 84 years earlier, Neptune had
held the honor of being the most
distant member of the far-flung
solar family.
The new object for some time
was designated by such names as
Planet X, the Flagstaff object and
the trans-Neptunian planet. Some
suggested that it should be called
Lowell after the late director of
the observatory since he had calculated that another planet must
lie beyond Neptune and had seemingly predicted its location fairly
accurately.

Girl Furnishes Name

Finally an 11-year-old girl, Venetia Burney of Oxford, England,
suggested to a noted astronomer
there that the new planet should be
called Pluto. Finally the suggestion was cabled to the Lowell observatory and the name was at
once adopted.
Pluto's average distance from
the sun is so great, 39.5 times that
of the earth, or nearly four billion miles out in the regions of
night, that the most powerful telescopes can make out nothing regarding its furnace features. Until
quite recently its size was estimated by little more than mere
guesses. It was thought to have
about the diameter of the earth,
or only slightly less. Brouwer at
Yale fairly recently estimated Pluto's mass at 0.9 times that of the
earth's.
In 1948 and 1949, Dr. Gerard
Kuiper of the University of Chicago attempted to measure fairly
accurately the diameter of Pluto
with the 82-inch telescope at the
McDonald observatory. In spite
of very careful manipulations he
felt sure for theoretical reasons
that the instrument was not delicate enough to measure such a
small angular diameter.

Nothing Accurate

On one occasion when the seeing
was especially good he and an assistant obtained a diameter of 0.4
second of arc, but he stated that
"the measurement was on the very
threshold of the capabilities of the
telescope—if not beyond it."
Early this year Dr. Kuiper arranged with the director of the
200-inch Hale telescope in California, for attempted measurements
with this the largest such instrument in operation. With the help
of Mr. Humason of the Palomar
staff, he was certain he obtained a
quite close result on the night of
March 22, 1950.
In the August issue of Publications of the Astronomical Society
of the Pacific Dr. Kuiper states
that his results give Pluto a diameter between that of Mars and

9451
SIZES
12–20

Here's a good nightie
dreaming! A good design
sewing too—see how
made. Do it with puff
now, no sleeves for sum
Style 9451: Sizes 12,
20. Size 16 takes 3½
inch; 4 yards 2¼-inch e
ing.
This easy-to-use style
fect fit. Complete, illus
chart shows you every s
The Marion Martin
book shows best-of
styles for all members o
ily, gives hints for gifts
make life easier for th
minded women.

Send 25 cents,
wrapped in paper, for
tern you want. Be sur
mistakes and order
terns advertised withi
year. If you wish a pat
enclose 25 cents addit
dress Spokane Daily
Pattern Department,
Wash. Order two wee
you want to use.—Ad

Points for Po
By EDYTHE WA

This

Mother: "Wouldn't y
buy dad's and my
your own money? W
small things you buy l
big ones we each buy
give to the other one.

* * *

Not Thi

Mother: "Jane seems
continue letting you p
the gifts she gives to
she should love us en
this herself, but I w
it to her."

Since then, the elite have been preparing behind the scenes building massive underground bases known as 'D.U.M.Bs' (deep underground military bases), sorting seeds of every plant species on the planet, cryogenically preserving species of the animal kingdom and been waging wars with anyone that doesn't agree to follow the 'new world order'.

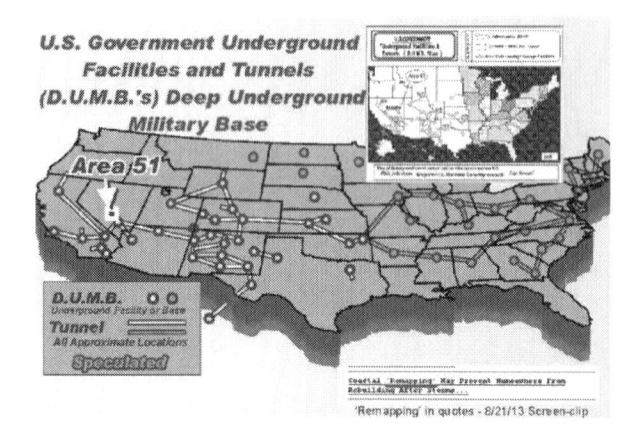

It's been the biggest cover up in human history...why? Because the very top elite know that the world would be put into absolute chaos overnight if they went public with this and they would have the biggest uprising in human history, their goals wouldn't be met so they keep you in a lower state of consciousness...keep watching the Kardashian's, 'nothing to see here' kind of thing.

Then you have to understand how the inclination of Earth plays a vital role in CERNs goals, Earth was locked in a 23-degree tilt for the few thousand years until around 7 years ago, when the system was within range to have an electromagnetic portal connection with all planets in our solar system.

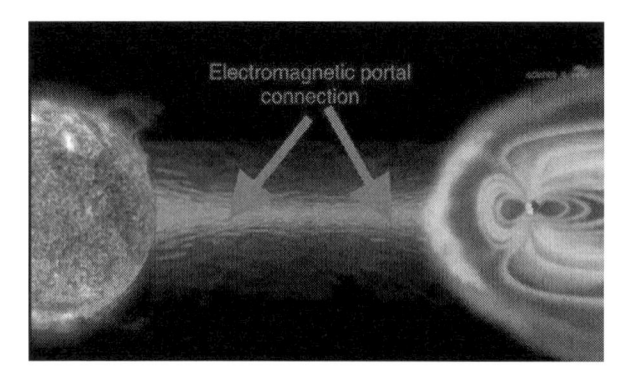

As we rotate around the sun each year, at one point of the year we pass the incoming system (still millions of miles away but it's extremely powerful) and as we pass it, magnetic repulsion takes place, our South Pole dips towards the system like two giant magnets battling forces, this in turn creates a 'Earth wobble' thus leading to the Earths inclination changing gradually which we monitor on the axis data charts, the Earth wobbles like a figure of 8, depending on where nibiru is on its orbit around its central star mass 'nemesis, one year nibiru could be the side of nemesis that Earths closest to as we past. The next year, nibiru could be the other side of nemesis away from

Earth as we pass it so the magnetic
interference is variable each year: -

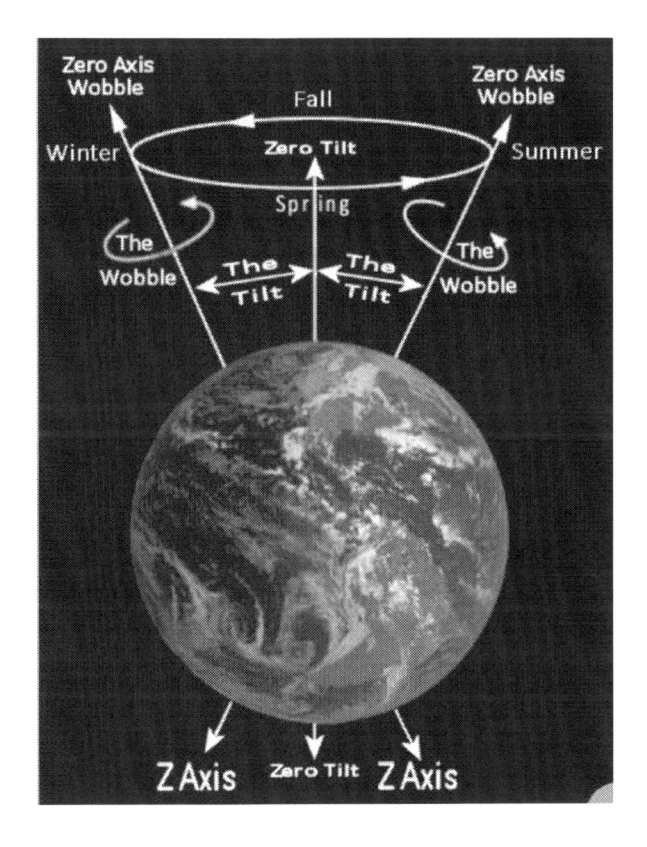

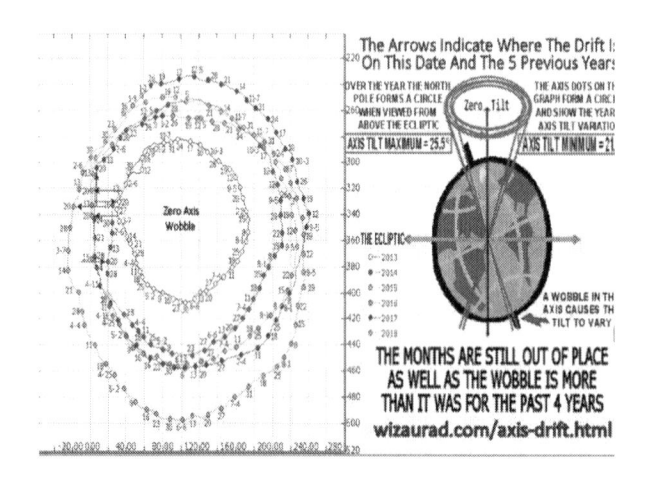

We monitor the data closely because the more the Earth wobbles, the weaker our magnetospheric protection becomes.

Along with that being said, they have underground cities/labs in Antarctica which is why you can't go to certain areas of Antarctica which is governed by a worldwide treaty, they also have an energy hub that runs all the way from Antarctica right up to the North Pole on the ocean floor, it's interconnected at both poles so they maximise the energy from the charged particles that come in on the solar wind. You can actually find the 'seabed wall' on google Earth but here's a video you can

search showing you it. https:-
//youtu.be/RPx5c8jIPSY and here's an image:
-

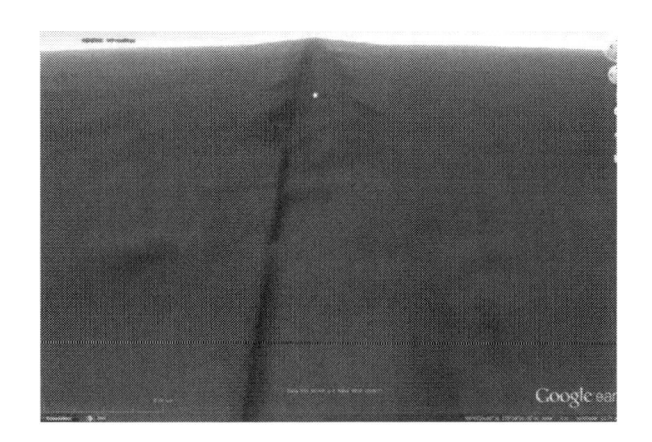

There is also a reason why the great pyramids of Giza are at the centre of all land mass and replicate the constellation 'Orion', as do the Mayan pyramids.

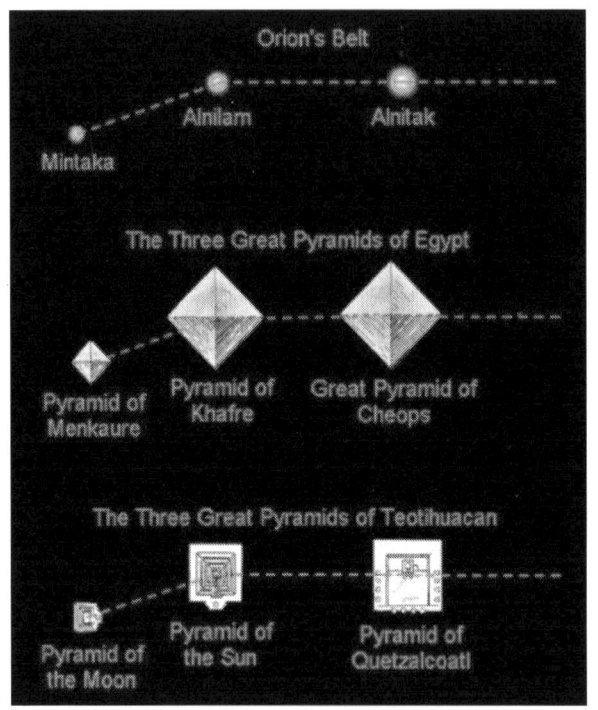

They were built to harness energy when certain planetary alignments occur, the tops of the pyramids are laced with crystals and granite which have impeccable abilities to store energy, just like every computer chipboard on the planet contain the same crystals to store information, very complex resource, even in the superman films they always used crystals: -

As always, they have to show you the truth in some way and if you compare the caves of Earth you will see the comparison: -

They also want to replicate the 'heavens' which is why they also use the term 'as above, so below' because nibiru is said to come from the constellation Orion, hence the replication of the pyramids.

The Anunnaki are referred to in the ancient Sumerian tablets profusely as the Gods, however, they are connected to the 'fallen angels' also who work with the underworld to make us a slave system as stated previously.

But not all are bad, there is more good than bad, however, the bad have the manipulation techniques to make us think the good are the minority, that's the way they want it, the elite depend on YOU needing THEM which is why they spread so much hate/divide/fear so that you feel the need to have them to keep things calm. Yet they do the opposite.

Each year the system gets closer, the more Earth inclination we see, it will swing one way for a while and then swing back the other way as our sun regains magnetic strength after we pass the system.

When 'nibiru' gets close enough to Earths orbital path it will come from directly under our South Pole, it is very hard to see because it's so far under the ecliptic, however, we have caught the system many times at the South Pole station, Neumeier: -

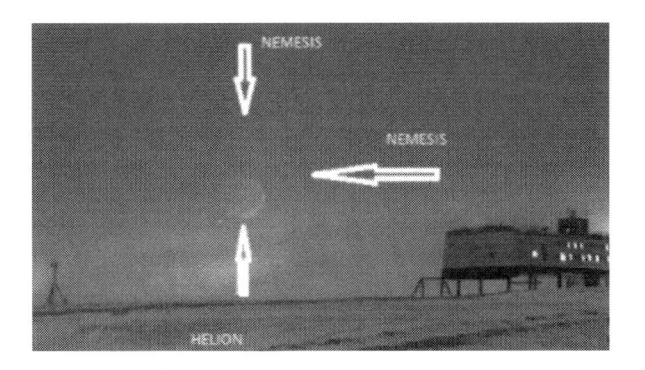

As the system rises from the ecliptic, the magnetic battle takes place, Earths South Pole will follow nibiru as it passes, that means our poles will shift, as they are shifting we will reach the '0' tilt.

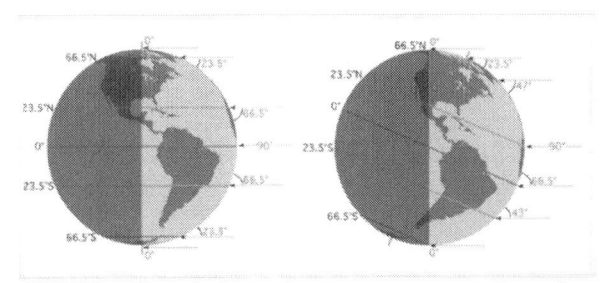

CERN will only have its most energy when the Earth is at '0' tilt due to the magnetosphere being at its most vulnerable, this means the charged particles will be entering our atmosphere at a faster rate, they can then harness that energy.

Do you see how it all connects?

CERN depends on plasma reactions.

our sun has been reacting to a second solar wind that interacts with the suns corona causing coronal holes: -

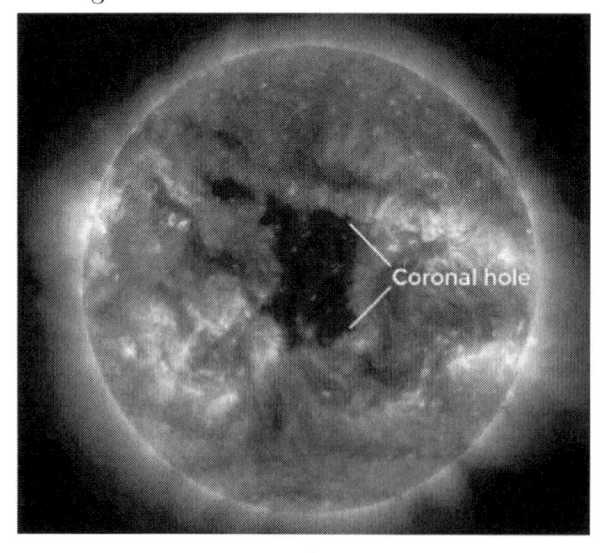

Also, the interaction creates large CMEs (coronal mass ejections) which create massive amounts of energy when Earth facing as they hit Earth through the solar wind: -

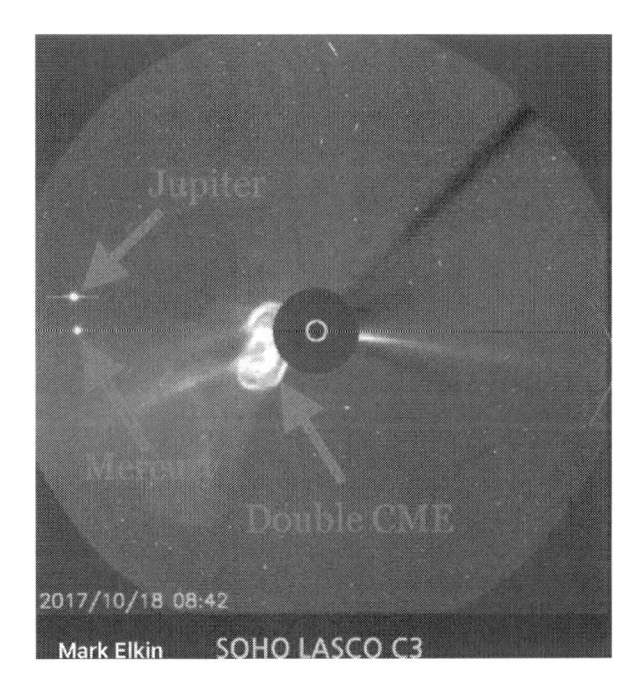

The charged particles get pulled in at the magnetic poles which is what creates the aurora: -

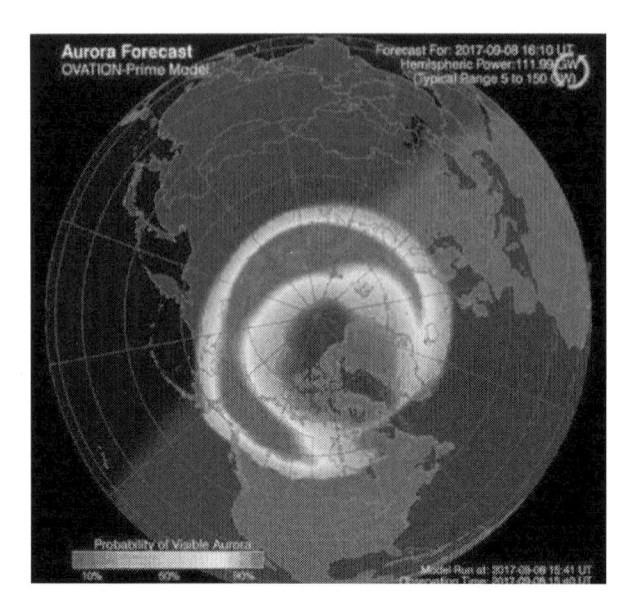

Then the particles spread through the ionosphere where the ionisation process takes place, CERN depend on plasma reactions and that's exactly what happens, that's why CERN always ramp up to max when we are expecting the arrival of a strong solar wind stream/CME, the timing is absolutely perfect.

This is why dolphins, whales and birds have been washing upon shores/falling out of the sky because the atmospheric compressions cause our magnetic field lines to be disrupted and they all navigate by using our magnetic field. Connect the dots: -

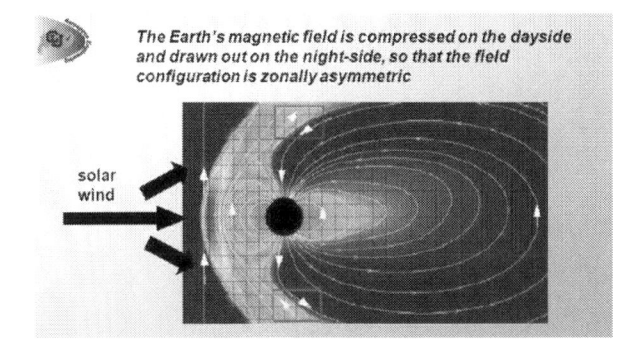

The Earth's magnetic field is compressed on the dayside and drawn out on the night-side, so that the field configuration is zonally asymmetric

The charged particles also interact with Earths plasmatic core, creating pressure under the plates which lead to Earthquakes, volcanic eruptions, sea temperature rise, ice cap reduction, landslides, sunk holes, tidal surges, hurricanes, tornados. All geological changes occur due to the core expansion through the magnetic influence in our solar system.

Here you can see how much the ice cap reduction is worsening: -

Arctic Sea Ice Extent
(Area of ocean with at least 15% sea ice)

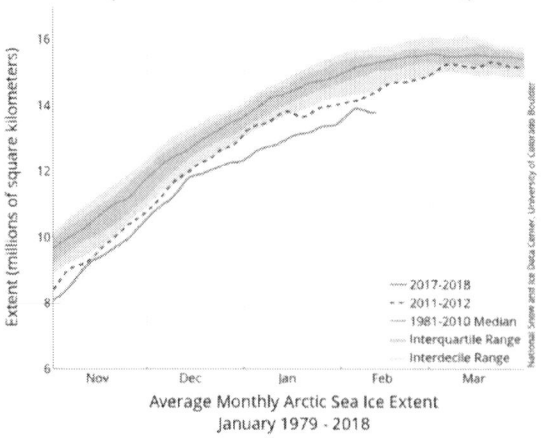

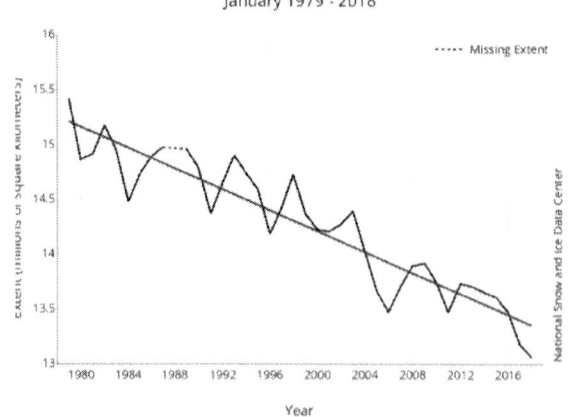

- 2017-2018
- 2011-2012
- 1981-2010 Median
- Interquartile Range
- Interdecile Range

National Snow and Ice Data Center, University of Colorado Boulder

Average Monthly Arctic Sea Ice Extent
January 1979 - 2018

- Missing Extent

National Snow and Ice Data Center

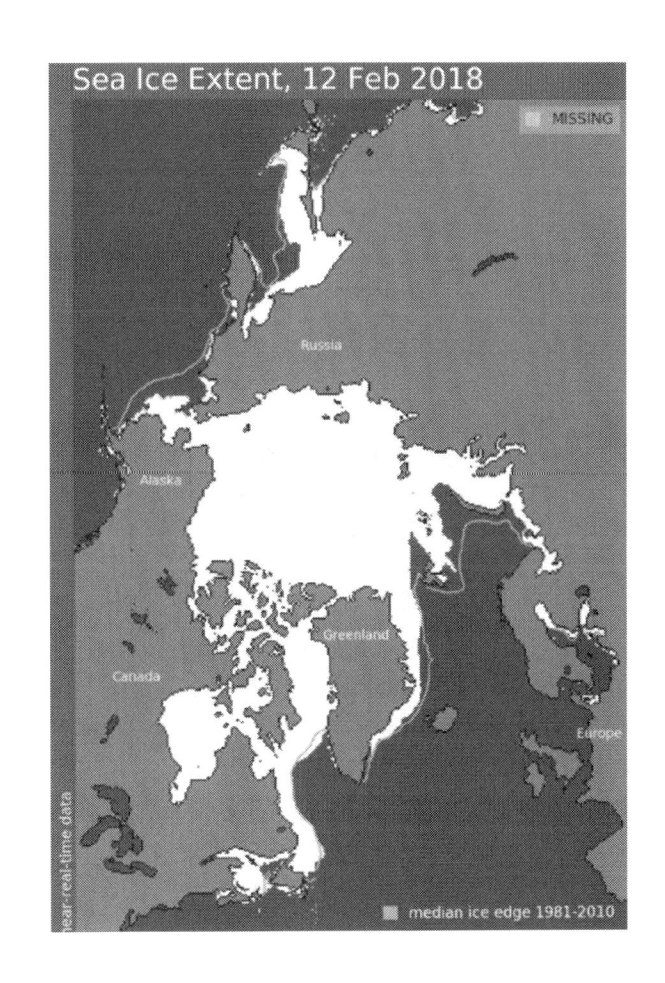

Sea Ice Extent, 12 Feb 2018

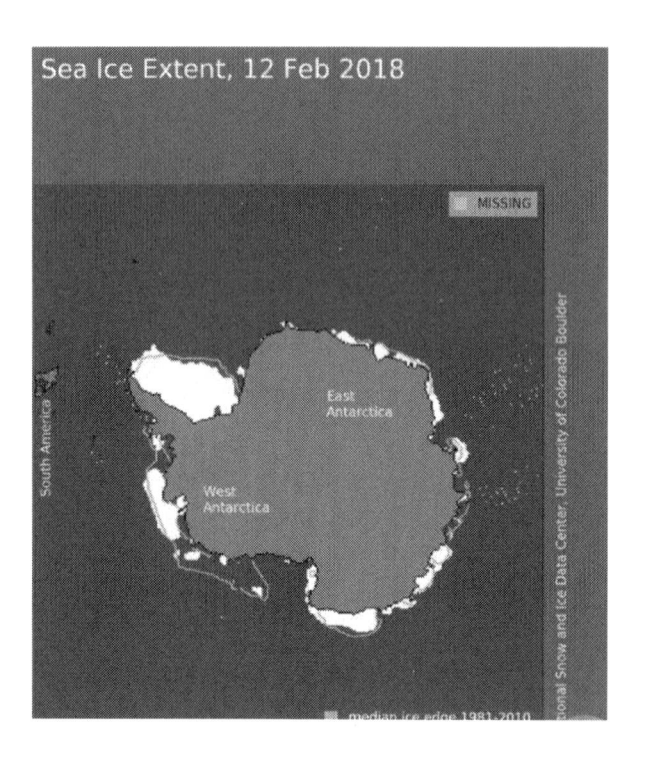

So, the closer the system gets to the proximity of our sun, the more interactions the sun has with Earth. The closer the system gets to Earths orbital path, the more Earth wobble we see, the more our jet streams intermix and the closer we get to the pole shift.

Which means the closer CERN get to their goal.

So, the elite know that they don't have long, they know they can't just get rid of millions of people without people noticing so they stage events and use weapons like D.E. Ws (direct energy weapons) to cause fires here's some patents and images so you get an idea of what DEWs are: -

129 STAT. 772   PUBLIC LAW 114-92—NOV. 25, 2015

(D) Projects and programs of the agencies and field activities of the Office of the Secretary of Defense that support business missions such as finance, human resources, security, management, logistics, and contract management.

(E) Military and civilian personnel policy development for information technology workforce.

10 USC 2501 note.

SEC. 218. DEPARTMENT OF DEFENSE TECHNOLOGY OFFSET PROGRAM TO BUILD AND MAINTAIN THE MILITARY TECHNOLOGICAL SUPERIORITY OF THE UNITED STATES.

(a) PROGRAM ESTABLISHED.—

(1) IN GENERAL.—The Secretary of Defense shall establish a technology offset program to build and maintain the military technological superiority of the United States by—

(A) accelerating the fielding of offset technologies that would help counter technological advantages of potential adversaries of the United States, including directed energy, low-cost, high-speed munitions, autonomous systems, undersea warfare, cyber technology, and intelligence data analytics, developed using research funding of the Department of Defense and accelerating the commercialization of such technologies; and

Santa Rosa, California

What type of 'forest fires' leave trees intact, but vaporize homes without a trace? Appliances, granite countertops, toilets, textiles, stonework etc completely vanished?

Firefighters reported "it's like we've been nuked", never seen anything like it. On the other hand, military intelligence agencies recently announced publicly that they've been testing directed energy weapons (DEW's) mounted to aircraft....

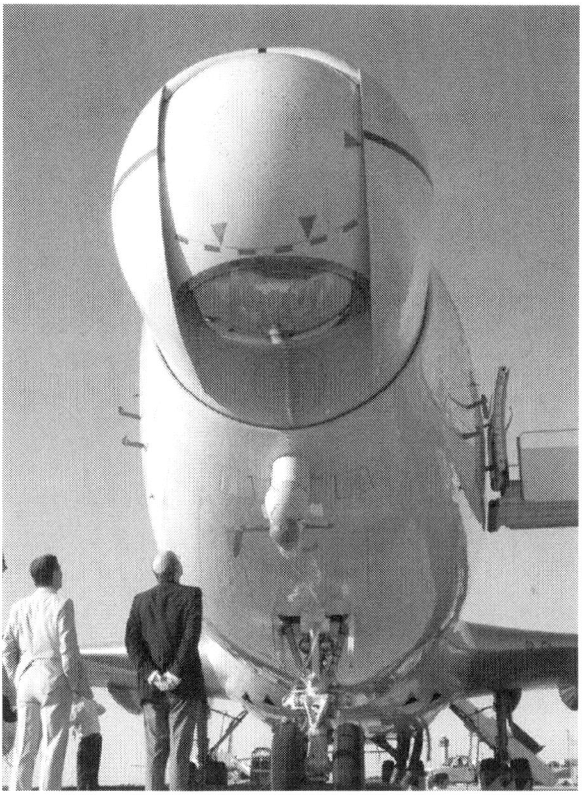

Directed energy weapon

WO2016024265A1
WO Application

🔍 Find Prior Art

Other languages: French

Inventor: Yehonatan SEGEV, Yochai SVIRSKY, Shay YUSOV, Yan ITOVICH

Original Assignee: Rafael Advanced Defense Systems Ltd.

Priority date: 2014-08-10

Family: US (1) WO (1)

Date	App/Pub Number	Status
2015-07-02	PCT/IL2015/050682	
2016-02-18	WO2016024265A1	Application

Abstract

The present invention relates to directed energy weapons and, in particular, it concerns directed energy weapons based on fiber lasers for use against a target, the weapon comprising: (a) a plurality of laser units, each of the laser units comprising: (i) a fiber laser generating an output beam from a fiber, the output beam conveying power of at least 1 kW, (ii) an objective lens arrangement for focusing the output beam into a focused beam directed towards the target, and (iii) a tine adjustment mechanism for adjusting a direction of the focused beam; (b) for each of the laser units, a beam deflector arrangement deployed to deflect a portion of the focused beam as a deflected beam in a direction in predefined relation to a direction of the focused beam; (c) an angle sensing unit deployed for receiving the deflected beams and generating an output indicative of a current direction of the deflected beam for each of the laser units; and (d) a controller associated with the angle sensing unit and the fine adjustment mechanisms, the controller being configured to actuate the fine adjustment mechanisms based on the output from the angle sensing unit to maintain a desired relative alignment between the directions of the focused beams.

Classifications

F41H13/0062 Directed energy weapons,

That's only few of the military grade weapons which is funded out of the 'black op' fund.

They have recently released a laser pen that can light a match with the beam itself so you can imagine how sophisticated the technology that military have is. Here's what you can buy for yourself: -

So, including the above, they also use **HAARP** to manipulate the hurricanes and steer them to the populated areas, they create Earthquakes (most are natural) to displace people and do the same with volcanoes.

This is all to round people up, separate as many of the gunslingers as possible (hence Obama taking people's guns which went against the second amendment), to put people in a position where they have no one else to go to apart from elite run organisations like 'FEMA' or 'UN' which is exactly what they want, then they have full control over you, the FEMA camps are systematically placed in areas that will be devastated by the pole shift. Do not go with FEMA/UN or any government-based agency when that time comes, do the opposite to what they are telling you to do on the television.

So, they depend on the pole shift, they need atmospheric compressions from the sun, they need the Earths tilt to alter to achieve their goals.

And all of the above is happening NOW.

The only step left is 'war of distraction' and 'project blue beam'.

They are the last and final stages of the 'new world order'.

If you here of 'aliens' all of a sudden coming to Earth then that's the moment you get the hell out of the cities/towns because that's when they will bring in 'martial law' and I mean worldwide. They have manmade crafts that can manipulate the electromagnetic forces around it to make it weightless, they can spin mercury around the exterior to make the central mass weightless and even have 'beings' that they have created for this event. They will use this to implement their 'one world religion', they will make it very bold in the mainstream media that the 'aliens' are here so most people will naturally turn to the elite for help, plays straight into their hands. These 'aliens' will be portrayed to be the 'Gods' and perform miracles all over the television screens which will fool the masses, it will all be manmade, designed to implement the final stage of the 'New World Order'. It is vital to not fall for this agenda. Here's a video you can search for just the basic released blue beam technology projections. So, you can image how sophisticated their technology's for when the event takes place. https://youtu.be/nsd6qVsefy4

95% of the world's population live near coastal areas.

The pole shift causes tidal surges that devastates the coastal areas with surges up to 1500ft.

The military will keep you where you are unwillingly by the coast because the elite have a completely different military which is funded out of the 'black op' fund so the normal military will be expendable I'm sorry to say.

They even tell you on the 'new world order' Georgia guide stones that they want to depopulate to 500 million people. There are 7.6 billion of us that are on this Earth.

Pole shift wipes out 95% of the worlds coastlines.

Connect the dots.

People will be easier to control in the after time if there are less people and will be easier to deceive for the 'one world religion'

Hence the importance of them creating false flags for martial law with project blue beam (fake alien invasion) being the biggest one of them all, the blue beam technology has been set up all round the world and is in place ready for the event, it's already been tested over less populated areas and it's made the local news headlines, which is the exact reaction people want, again, do not fall for it.

The pole shift itself cannot be stopped, it's like a cleanse of the Earth and has happened many times before throughout history and is well documented.

But what you can stop from happening is letting the elite use their frequency manipulators to control you.

Be positive, don't let things scare you, you have the ability to live above all of the negativity they emit purposely and all you have to do is change your thought process, be happy, be caring, be loving. Do absolutely everything in your power to be compassionate, you do that, the rest will take care of itself.

This brings me to the cartoon series 'the Simpsons' which has heavy ties to the occult and the pole shift.

Just remember, evil has many faces. People think that trump is in power because the people put him there, it doesn't work like that and people should be cautious to think someone with that much money and greed was put in place for good reasons.

Trump is in the elite, it was planned for him to go in to power, just like they said he would in the Simpsons.

Remember that the Simpsons was created and directed by Matt Groening who is a 33rd degree high priest mason: -

That itself should get alarm bells ringing, the Simpsons has predicted a lot of events that have unfolded because the elite stick to strict plan, as always, they stick to their agenda and by the universal law, they have to subliminally show us the events before they happen, this is fact.

This is how the illuminati works, Trump always does the '6' sign in all his speeches which to some means nothing, to people who study symbolism know that this is him showing his respects to his higher power, it's never a coincidence, they will publicly do these hand gestures on purpose and always have done: -

It's all part of the plan and this is all relevant as you can tell by now after reading previous chapters.

Now these next set of still shots you'll see what the Simpsons have predicted way before the events took place, from the Ebola virus, 911 to the coming pole shift. As always- the truth is stranger than fiction.

Season 9, in an episode called 'Lisa's sax' which first aired on October 19th 1997 clearly shows them portraying the Ebola virus, even though the Ebola virus was recognised before 1997 it still doesn't equate to why they would add this in their series whilst showing Bart becoming ill from the virus whilst Marge shows him a book about the Ebola virus, which has led many to believe that the elite are showing you that the Ebola virus was going to be a widespread disease: -

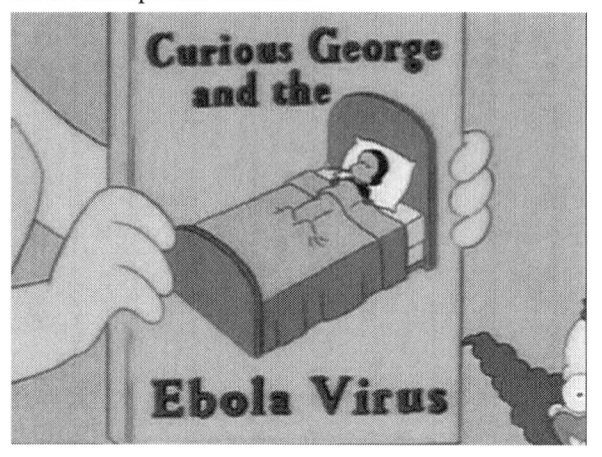

But the Ebola virus prediction is a minor one considering that they have predicted a much more well-known conspiracy known as '911'. In the episode 'New York City Against Homer', Lisa holds up a magazine with the word New York accompanied by a number nine against a silhouette of the World Trade Centre – which makes the number 11: -

The design is a direct reference to 9/11.

The episode was first aired in September 1997, a full four years before the terrorist atrocities in the Big Apple when the world trade centre towers came crumbling down.

To add to the 911 conspiracy, here is a few other references that is pictured in images years before the attack occurred: -

Johnny Bravo - "Chain Gang Johnny" (April 27, 2001)

Asi sufre Latino America" (1983)

Beavis and Butthead - Vice Magazine (1994)

Illuminati: - The Game of Conspiracy cards

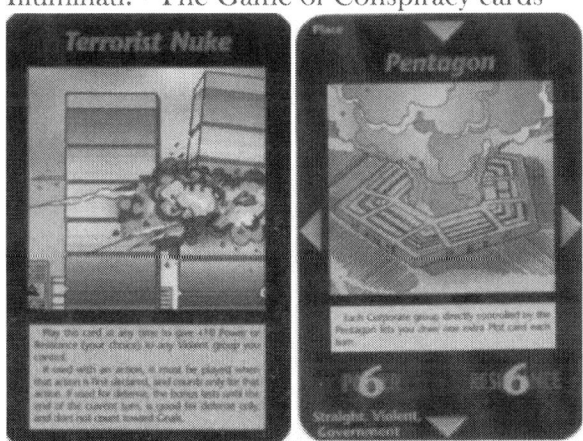

(Early '80s)

Marvel Comic Book (1983). Nazis are part of the illuminati, all run by the Jesuit Masonic realms, all the same people.

PIA Advertisement (1979)

Terminator 2 (1991)

Those are just a few subliminal messages in films/adverts, there are hundreds of them but by now I think you can figure out the bigger picture; as always, they have to show you in some form of what's going to happen before it does.

Back to the Simpsons; they have made a lot of other predictions, as in the FIFA scandal, the German World Cup victory, FaceTime, Roy's tiger attack, faulty voter machines, the God particle (CERN), Greece's dent default, autocorrection, smart watches, the NSA snooping on US citizens and, most unbelievable at the time, the Rolling Stones still touring in 2010.

The one prediction that stands out for most researchers is in Season 11, Episode 17: - 'Bart to the Future' in 2000 where it predicts that Donald trump will be the US president: -

Came true in 2016.

As you can gather, there is a much deeper meaning to all these predictions, how do they know the events are going to happen before they happen? Because it's all orchestrated by the elite to gain control over Earth for their 'one world government' where innocent people die in order to achieve their agenda, to gain as much control as possible before the 'Pole shift'.

Which leads me to the most important Simpsons episode to date, considering all over predictions have come true I would advise the reader to take this fully on board, the episode is called 'days of futures past' and clearly shows a pole shift: -

This clearly portrays the Empire State Building being completely submerged under water, which would be the outcome of the pole shift, but it doesn't stop there: -

As you can see, this clearly portrays the South Pole being a hot dessert area which would only occur if Earth was to go through a pole shift, coincidence? Well, if you judge it on what you have already seen previously, I think you would agree that this is much more than a coincidence and more of a prophecy yet to be for filled.

The Simpsons not only predict the pole shift but they also predict what it would be like after the pole shift has occurred; they portray that there will be a very big difference in society, the people that follow the government will be chipped but will be made to feel like a higher class, even though they will be under more control and government even more in the elites matrix, whereas the people that don't follow the elite will be classed as the 'outcasts' of society, the elite will brainwash the 'higher class' people into thinking we are nothing but savages, thieves, murdering hordes of ruthless animals when in reality; we will be the ones that are peaceful, the people that want the best for Mother Earth, the people that don't want to be shackled under the system that they want to imprison us in, the people that are of good, kind, caring, compassionate nature. The people that the elite hate due to them having no control over our God given right to be free.

This image shows the 'outcasts' that they will class us as: -

This image shows how the 'upper class' of society have all the new technology in the after time of the shift, how they have chips to go through a dimensional portal door to get across the planet: -

However, Lisa's chip doesn't work so is forced to travel with the 'outcasts' of society: -

So that is showing you how they want it after everything has settled, if the remaining people don't agree with 'the new world order' or 'one world religion' then you will be an outcast fighting for survival.

CHAPTER 4

FREQUENCIES, SOUND AND YOU.

The world is going through a transition, it's up to you how you let it affect you.

I'm only here to show you truth and help you protect your physical body through the geological changes of Earth, your spirituality is in your hands and only you can change it.

Remember, you are just a sound wave, a vibration, a frequency. Nothing is truly solid, everything is made up of practically empty particles held together by the synchronicity of our perception.

You are the universe, don't let them make you think that you're not.

Mainstream scientists have manipulated the children of the masses through their agendas for the elite, they have portrayed that the universe was created through a 'big bang'.

For there to be a Big Bang, things would have to exist to birth a creation of life, life meaning energy itself. What is energy? Well it's merely a vibrational frequency on the physical realm of our perception, meaning; everything around you is in perfect synchronicity with what you see.

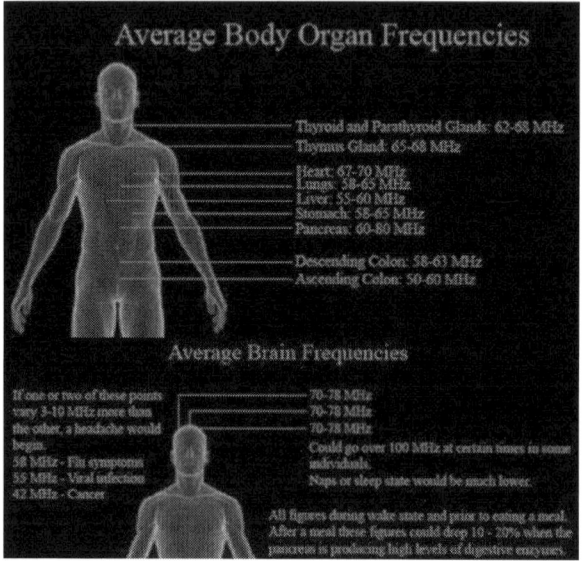

Average Body Organ Frequencies

- Thyroid and Parathyroid Glands: 62-68 MHz
- Thymus Gland: 65-68 MHz
- Heart: 67-70 MHz
- Lungs: 58-65 MHz
- Liver: 55-60 MHz
- Stomach: 58-65 MHz
- Pancreas: 60-80 MHz
- Descending Colon: 58-63 MHz
- Ascending Colon: 50-60 MHz

Average Brain Frequencies

- 70-78 MHz
- 70-78 MHz
- 70-78 MHz

If one or two of these points vary 3-10 MHz more than the other, a headache would begin.
58 MHz - Flu symptoms
55 MHz - Viral infection
42 MHz - Cancer

Could go over 100 MHz at certain times in some individuals.
Naps or sleep state would be much lower.

All figures during wake state and prior to eating a meal. After a meal these figures could drop 10 - 20% when the pancreas is producing high levels of digestive enzymes.

This means that the tiniest of particles react differently when not being observed, this means atoms or the things that make up atoms like electrons/neutrons/protons etc have an actual conscience, the simple 'double slit' experiment proves that so, hence the common phrase *"if quantum physics hasn't scared you yet, you don't understand it"*

NUCLEUS — **PROTON** — **NEUTRON** — **ELECTRON**

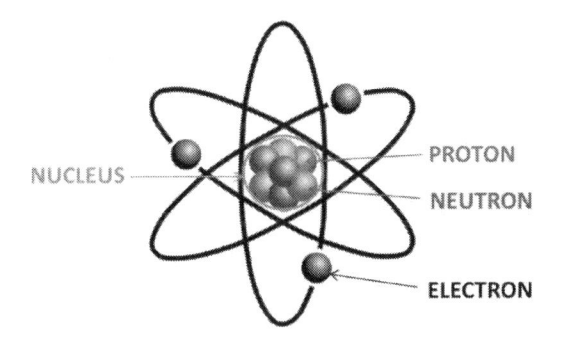

If a tree falls in the Forrest but there is no one there to hear it, does it make a sound? Well if the tiniest particles that make up every piece of matter on Earth change the way they act when being observed how would anyone possibly be able to answer that question?

In fact, atoms are practically empty space, literally nothingness but it becomes a solid mass in conjunction with our perception..think about that for a second.

Everything you see is only a perceptive dimensional state of consciousness, we used to have a completely different state of consciousness, a higher connection with the universe, astral travel was the normal thing before the elite found ways of manipulating the frequencies that work with our perception.

The ancient civilisations knew how to work with the multi-dimensional universe we live in, the universe we know today is merely just the universe you've been trained to perceive.

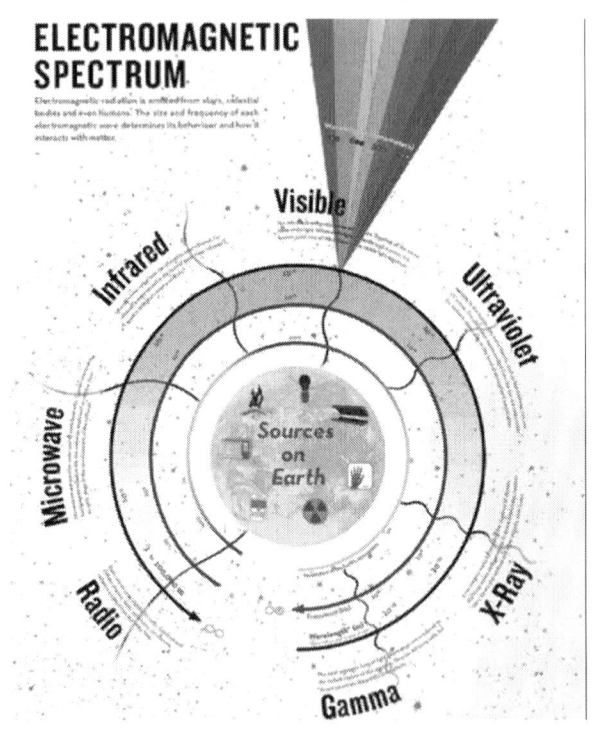

We live in a multiverse, we have interred dimensional races that can perceive different vibrational planes.

There is a reason we cannot see all the colours of the spectrum and there is a reason why we cannot hear certain sound waves, it's because they are in a different dimension.

You are made up of the exact same things that make up our known universe- energy

Energy cannot be destroyed, impossible.

Your energy=your soul

Your soul=spiritual vibrational frequency. Our existence didn't happen by chance, it is intricate, specific, intelligent design from a creation of a creator.

Some people think we are just a bunch of atoms that was ironically created from a combusted cloud of fusion...it's far too complex and would make more sense if we were in an intelligent computer simulation, which we are not but we are in a very intelligent format of design.

It's hard explaining these concepts to mainstreamer humans but if you research it all yourself in depth it will all start making sense- everything.

Start with Tesla, he had a great understanding of the universe and was consciously connected to the vibrational frequencies of the cosmos, he figured out how to implement free energy from using the 'ether' and connect through the electromagnetic field of Earth. The elite swiftly closed him down so that they could still continue to make the masses pay for power. All for control.

He had the understanding of the following-

3,6,9
Golden ratio
Sacred geometry
Quantum physics
Flower of life
Electromagnetism
Sound
Vibration
Light
Ether
Frequencies
Metatrons cube

This is nothing to do with religion, I'm not religious.

Religion was created to wage wars and divide. This is all about your consciousness, your dimensional state.

Be good, kind and spiritual...that's all you need.

Think of all the millions of kids that go missing yearly, not only do the elite drink the blood of the young but they also do rituals in Satan's name, who's Satan? The king of the fallen angels. They have interred dimensional capabilities hence way all the magicians have a tattoo of an all-seeing eye (illuminati): -

because they know how to invoke the powers of underworld through a different dimension...just like Solomon, the knights templar found something in his temple that made them very powerful, what was it? Some think it's the holy grail yet it was merely just black magic capabilities which again, invoke the powers of the negative realms which is why just a handful of knights Templars would turn up to battle with the opposite side having hundreds of men yet the hundreds would run in terror...it's all to do with sacred geometries and how to manipulate our perceptive dimensional state and allow other dimensions to be seen ...it's hard to explain and hard to understand I know but Satan is the ruler of Earth, he craves flesh and blood...

There has to be balance you see, one thing we all have is 'free will', Satan can only entice you to follow the lower realms through power/greed/wealth but it's our choice to follow that way of life or not but that's for your SOUL, to be kept in his lower, much darker frequency of dimension.

Hence why 'love' is the key to the universe because of vibrational dimension it surrounds you. This is why they kill people like bob Marley/john Lennon etc because they spread love and if lots of people listen to their music all the time then it raises their consciousness into a higher state, a good vibrational dimension.

The elite want the opposite, things like 'tomorrow land' the music festival, you'll see how demonic it is and they feed off the energy that is given at the festival so the dark forces gain the energy: -

The music videos of Rihanna/jay z/Justin Bieber etc always have demonic symbolism in their videos and use the lower frequency band to play their music thus surrounding most of the world in the negative vibrational frequency: -...do you see how deeply well thought out all this is now? Crazy right but once it clicks it's the most important thing you'll ever learn: -

Wonder why the illuminati use a triangle? Hexagram? Pentagram? Because that's the negative frequency pattern in the geometry.

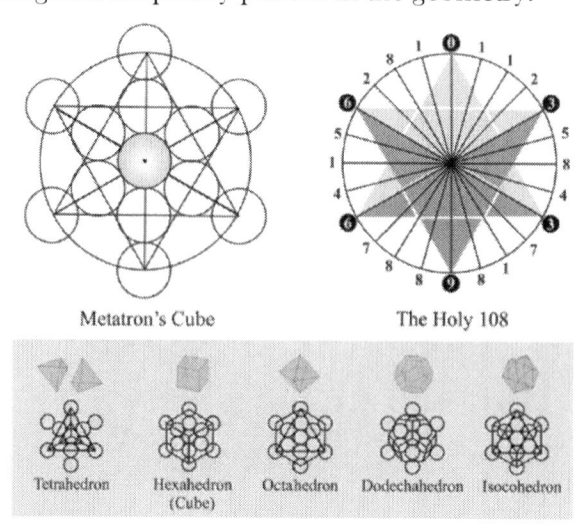

Metatron's Cube

The Holy 108

Tetrahedron   Hexahedron (Cube)   Octahedron   Dodechahedron   Isocohedron

A Metatron's cube contains all the carbon Platonic solids, all them solids are frequencies/vibration which make a certain pattern through sound ....in other words- they represent the dark negative dimension of the metatrons cube, the metatrons cube is a part of a certain frequency that makes up our known universe/multiverse which contains our dimension/dark dimension/positive dimension and so on...the metatrons cube also is part of the 'flower of life' geometric frequency which is a frequency that entails our entire cosmos, universe, multiverse:-

The flower of life is symmetric, geometric symbol that represents all life, solid mass, sacred symbolism, universal electromagnetic wave forms. All frequencies are within the flower of life.

Once it hits you it's like a eureka moment.

So, for people to die, starve etc this is all because of The underworld .9/11 was a huge occult ritual, killing in Satan's name, these things are well planned and thought out because that's when Jesus was actually born so everything is an inversion to Jesus.

Why are these things happening? Because the creator said it would. Fish dying/birds dying/famine/wars and rumours of wars/mass land animals die offs/Earthquakes/floods/volcanic eruptions.

Everything that the bible/scriptures/ancient carvings/ancient paintings/cuneiform tablets etc warned us of...this is God's word- 'end days'

Look at Earth, look how unholy it's become? Thousands of years ago people were connected to the universe, now the dark hand in charge prevents that from happening and pushes sex/drugs/money all over the mind programmer- TELEVISION. (look up patent number US 6506148 B2).: -

Nervous system manipulation by electromagnetic fields from monitors

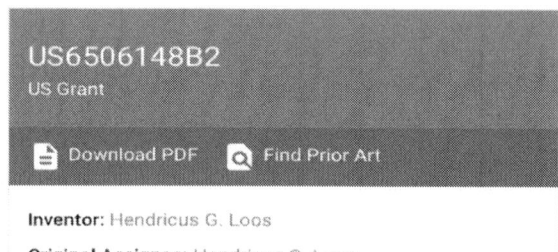

US6506148B2
US Grant

Download PDF   Find Prior Art

Inventor: Hendricus G. Loos
Original Assignee: Hendricus G. Loos
Priority date: 2001-06-01

Abstract

Physiological effects have been observed in a human subject in response to stimulation of the skin with weak electromagnetic fields that are pulsed with certain frequencies near ½ Hz or 2.4 Hz, such as to excite a sensory resonance. Many computer monitors and TV tubes, when displaying pulsed images, emit pulsed electromagnetic fields of sufficient amplitudes to cause such excitation. It is therefore possible to manipulate the nervous system of a subject by pulsing images displayed on a nearby computer monitor or TV set. For the latter, the image pulsing may be imbedded in the program material, or it may be overlaid by modulating a video stream, either as an RF signal or as a video signal. The image displayed on a computer monitor may be pulsed effectively by a simple computer program. For certain monitors, pulsed electromagnetic fields capable of exciting sensory resonances in nearby subjects may be generated even as the displayed images are pulsed with subliminal intensity.

Images (10)

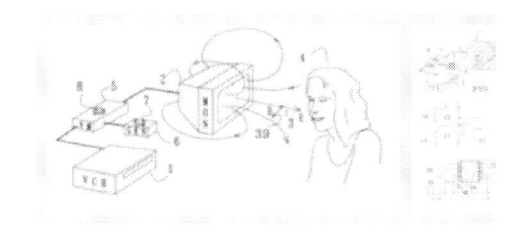

This has turned the world in to a horrible place, science is underworlds biggest weapon for this is what pushed everyone away from their natural understanding of our multiverse 'and he was blinded by science'

We are living in the end times as we speak, it's our ancestors fault for falling for the underworlds offer of science, this is what led to everything that's all around you today, unnatural surroundings.

But there is always a fight between good and evil, the good will use science to benefit humans, make people walk again, heart surgery, cure diseases. Whereas the negative realm use science to build bombs, create diseases, manipulate the weather and so on. Always a battle, it's your choice which side you choose, that's your free will.

Think about it, we chop down millions of trees every year, the one thing that connects all living things on Earth and biggest source of oxygen...is that because we want to? No, it's because the public have been gradually brainwashed into thinking it's normal and 99% of the world population don't even care so again, the mind manipulation from the negative frequencies win.

Still got a long way to go before tranquillity returns, the build up to the crossing is the crossing of the planets and the crossing itself is the 'tribulations' spoke of in scripture.

So, if we are looking to blame God/universe/creator we must first think about who really is to blame- science, humans free will to accept the negative science that's been shown to us.

The powers that are in charge of Earth are pure evil...our creator cares for your soul and will only get it through staying true to the kindness of yourself, not tempted by all the negative energy that brings false/temporary comfort.

It's all one big battle, it's how you fight in the battle that determines your souls resting place, not whether you die in the flesh.

So, Jesus was very real, he was able to be connected to a higher frequency which is a higher state of consciousness which is also a different dimensional state thus being more connected to the creator/multiverse/other dimensions...was he chosen to spread love? Well of course. He was sent here to warn us all of the bad doings that are happening now.

'Love' is the key to multiverse because 'love' gives off a vibration that overpowers all negativity and Jesus knew that, he gave the masses a choice whether to follow his ways, that's the choice everyone has, it's your 'free will' that determines the energy you surround yourself in, totally.

if you are negative and full of hate then you surround yourself in that negative dimension of frequencies, you attract the negative vibrations that will begin to synchronise with the energy waves your giving off, it's as simple as that so the elite do everything in their power to make this happen...i.e. Cost of living/death on the media/mass shootings/bombing/video games/music. All of it is controlled by the elite which has a negative effect on the masses consciousness...

This is their matrix; the only way out is to be positive/non-judgmental/kind/loving/compassionate

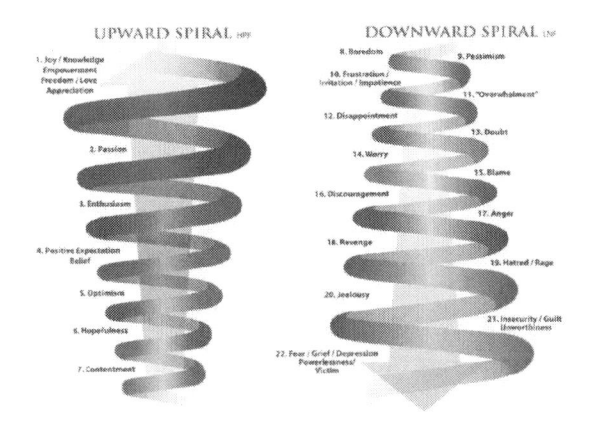

Because if you're the opposite, the elite have already won.

It's all about sound/vibration/frequencies...we only see this specific dimension that's completely synchronised to our perception.

There are many dimensions, so think about what dimension you want to surround yourself in.

You're not born racist, you're taught to be.

You're not born with any religion, you're taught to be religious.

Think about that...

"Love conquers all"

These are the most important things to understand, these are the elements that are the building blocks of the universe.

 In complete symmetry, these are the exact same things that make up **YOU**.

Start with vibration, which is the beginning of everything

'Let there be light'

Light is a frequency...

Frequency is a vibration...

Once you understand all of the above, you will never look at life the same.

You will still be you, you will still live everyday as it was the same but at the same time, your consciousness will be completely different.

Your consciousness is part of the universe.

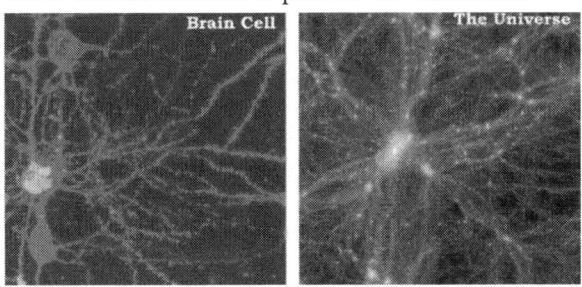

You have the ability to connect to it, your physical realm is just one of the frequencies that totally synchronise with your perception. As previously stated, but it's so important to understand.

Which means every known atom (electron, proton, neutron) which makes up absolutely everything in the physical realm react to the way you perceive it.

Hard to digest, even the smallest particles on the planet have a consciousness...even time travel is proven through the 'double slit' experiment (if researched enough) - (they don't like people knowing about this).

This destroys the equation of 'relativity' - Einstein of course, clever man, still just a theoretical scientist which is still taught in schools unfortunately.

The mathematical equation of a black hole is infinity x infinity reoccurring, which proves relativity is completely flawed, which means gravity is completely flawed, which means 'matter' is completely flawed.

Could you imagine if they went globally public about the quantum world all of a sudden? It would mean that every scholar that's been taught would be passing their scientific exams on a false narrative?! How would the educated teachers/scientists/astrophysicists etc be able to redeem themselves? That's why they bring technologies forward slowly and pretend to have found new particles with incredible energy even though these energies have been used for millennials.

Impossible, that's why the scientists that was taught by the scientists before them will always be taught the same science, it's a knock-on effect on the theory that's taught just because it fits in with the achievements of old science.

That's why the same science is always taught until you get to certain universities where some new science enthusiasts try to explain the quantum mechanics of particles.

Hard to digest for all the Einstein's/Edison's/or NASA enthusiasts out there and only 2% of the world population want to know about New science so hardly anyone in this planet knows the real science nor the advanced science the elite use.

It's indoctrinated into the education system that black is black, white is white, physics is physics, atoms are atoms and matter are matter.

We are much more than just tiny little particles all joined together through atomic fusion, we are part of the universe, we are the universe, there is no such thing as nothing, everything is interconnected through constant flows of energy.

Some people are connected through the frequencies of good, love and truth.

Some people are connected through the evil that surrounds them- bad, evil, fear, anger, rage and sadness.

But it's our own free will which frequencies we surround ourselves in.

You will always have a choice. Good or bad, right from wrong...that defines who you become as a 'person' which is your 'personality' which is the 'consciousness'.

You create your own surroundings, it's totally your choice, free will, your personal reality is what you make of your own.

'Life is what you make it'

Never a truer word spoken.

You think negative, you surround yourself in negative frequencies.

You see the good in everything? You surround yourself in positive frequencies.

It really is that simple, your actions/reactions create the surroundings you live in.

You know who the elite like to communicate with now, the lower frequencies, this is why they try to lower your own frequency. Don't let them do it. See the good in everything, be happy, be loving, be kind, be compassionate and be free.

Prime example of how this works- let's say you are sitting in a room surrounded by solid brick walls...your WIFI box is in the next room. Your laptop/PC/mobile phone is connected to that WIFI box which allows you to use the internet. Yet there is a solid mass in the way between your device and the WIFI box? How does this work? Well, the wall isn't truly solid; it's merely made up of a certain vibrational frequency. Whereas your WIFI connection is a completely different frequency which means it can literally go through the 'solid' wall as if it didn't even exist. Different dimensions.

Same goes for this; I want the reader to take a moment here and try to test this out- I want you to say a sentence in your mind, you can say absolutely anything you want but you must not say anything out loud, only using your mind, for example: - "I want to go to the shop today" but without orally making any kind of sound...3,2, 1...go! You can do this a couple of times if it helps. Now, you will hear yourself say these words yet you didn't make any sort of sound whatsoever so how did you hear it? For you to hear something a sound wave has to synchronise with your eardrums but you still heard it without a sound being made? How does that work? It's because your consciousness is connected to different vibrational frequencies, different dimensions, your consciousness is part of a multi-dimensional highway.

There are certain 'laws' of the universe which cannot be manipulated and even the entities of most high have to abide to.

In the book 'why the New World Order will fail by author 'Marc Gielissen', he explains these laws with brilliant clarity;

(According to the Kybalion (which is the study of The Hermetic Philosophy of Ancient Egypt and Greece), first published in 1908 under the pseudonym of "the Three Initiates", and "The Science of being", written by Baron Eugene

Fersen in 1923, we have seven major universal laws. It is important to understand them in order to know why we are going through this period and what will happen to us, explained in a later phase in this book. Our Universe is governed by seven Universal laws, principles or axioms. All in perfect harmony and balance by virtue of these laws. Within the seven laws we can define three that are immutable (Meaning that they can never be changed) and four that are transitory (They can be transcended or changed). 1 The law of mentalism (Immutable) All what we see or experience in the physical world has its origin in the mental realm. It is very important to understand the principals, because it shows us that we have a single Universal Consciousness. We could call it the "Universal mind", from where all energy and matter is created. We are all interconnected, every individual's mind is part of the universal mind. Your reality is first created in your mind and then manifested in the material world. Basic principle: - "All is mind"

2 The law of correspondence (immutable) It tells us that; "as above, so below and as below so above." There is agreement between the spiritual, physical and mental realms. We are all part of the one source, therefore there is no

separation. It is a pattern that exists from the smallest electron to the biggest star and it is not changeable. The 3 realms being; The great Physical realm the great Mental realm the great Spiritual realm Basic principle: - "As above, so below: -as below, so above"

3 The law of vibration (Immutable) Everything is in movement all the time and everything around us vibrates and circles, including our own body. This law tells us that the whole Universe consist of vibration. All things, including we humans, are pure energy and vibrating, although at different frequencies. All our thoughts and emotions are vibrations. When we look at emotions, we know that unconditional love will be the absolute highest and hate the absolute lowest or most dense vibration. Basic principle: - "Nothing rests, everything moves, vibrates and circles"

4 The law of polarity (Mutable) It tells us that everything has its pair of opposites, everything is dual and has poles. Love and hate, positive and negative, energy and matter. People often say that love and hate are close, it's very true as it only takes a person to raise his or her vibration to change hate into love. There are always two sides to everything in the Universe.

Basic principle: - "everything is and isn't at the same time"

5 The law of rhythm (Mutable) All things will flow out and flow back in, best to be compared with the swing of a pendulum, where the momentum of right swing will create that of the left swing. We see it in the tides of the sea and even whole civilizations that rise and fall. Understanding this law will be very important for humanity, as it will help us to bend negative thoughts into positive thoughts and by doing so we create a new reality. It is closely related to the law of polarity. Basic principle: - "Flow and inflow"

6 The law of cause and effect (Mutable) It tells us that every cause has its effect and every effect has his cause. Every single thought, action or even words are created in your mental or inner world, they will set a specific effect in motion that will materialise over time. In my first book "Roots in the Congo", I explained this phenomenon by citing different examples in life were the "power of thought" resulted in the desired outcome. Basic principle: - "There is no chance, only cause and effect"

7 The law of gender (Mutable) Everything has masculine and feminine principles in the Universe. It is present in opposite sexes found in humans, but also in minerals, magnetic poles, electrons etc. It also means that everyone and everything has a masculine and feminine side. For humans this means that in every woman lies the qualities of a man and for any man the qualities of a woman. This is not related to sexuality, only spirituality. Basic principle: - "Mental gender manifests as feminine and masculine sides in all realms" Later on in this publication, we will understand why I elaborated on the laws of the universe and why they are a necessary part of this book. Humanity has made many mistakes in the past, but is on a major crossroad today, ready to change direction. A completely new era, which will change everything we currently experience and know, it will reveal itself to us when the time is right. Humanity will raise the vibrational level in order to enter the new realm of peace and love. A realm or plane in which no more armies will be necessary and people will live by the power of the Universe and the One creator or God.)

I have to agree, as a collective, we will reach the high realms of consciousness after the pole shift occurs. The 'Schumann resonance' is spiking continuously as the system draws closer which in turn, creates a certain frequency that interacts with our consciousness.

It doesn't work for everyone, only the good people, the kind hearted, the people that are meant to 'wake up' will start to see signs in their own self, for example; you may hear humming in your ears, feel sensitive, emotional, become more caring with nature, start to feel like you don't fit in with the everyday crowds. You will start having vivid dreams. Many signs that you might not even realise are happening to you for any particular reason are actually the biggest reason of your life so embrace it all.

I highly recommend reading 'why the New World Order will fail by Marc Gielissen, it gives a very in-depth explanation of how you can raise your consciousness and also speaks of the coming events, including nibiru. He also has a very active Facebook group called; 'Exposing the New World Order' where people give daily insights to spiritual awareness and Earth change updates. They focus on the positive, in a very negative world.

The key to the universe is 'love', it's the highest form of frequency you can connect to and you are being shown these things for a reason, you are reading this because we are already connected through strings of truth which the universal energy has provided for us, this means you are meant to survive the coming events to carry on the human race with the loving nature we are meant to have and serve, so take heart in knowing that.

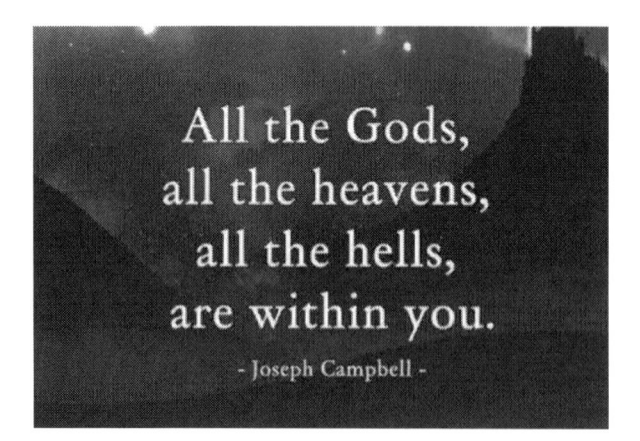

> All the Gods,
> all the heavens,
> all the hells,
> are within you.
>
> - Joseph Campbell -

CHAPTER 5

GEOLOGICAL/SOLAR CHANGES LEADING UP TO THE POLE SHIFT.

Here I will explain the science behind the effects of the incoming system, the particle interaction, the plasma reactions, the suns solar wind stream, geomagnetic storms and so on.

First of all, we have to take a look how our suns solar wind stream interacts with the cosmic particles of the incoming system and how it affects all geological changes on Earth.

Below I will give reference to the 'ACE' satellite which measures the particle stream that comes towards Earth from the suns solar wind. I will give explanations for each section so the reader can learn what each colour represents and how it effects Earth: -

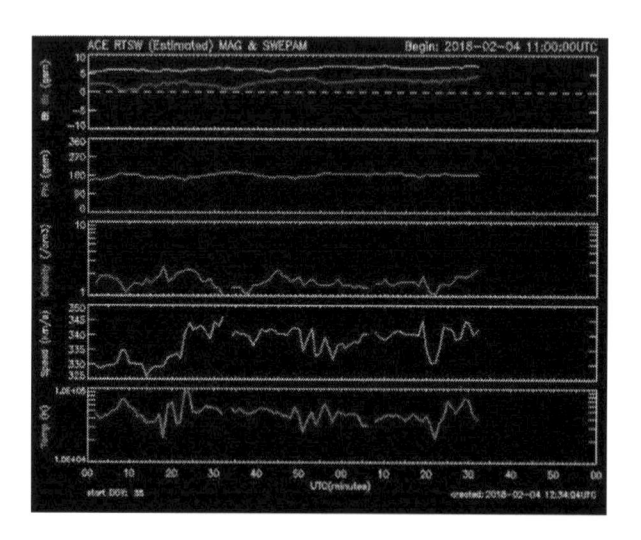

Wind Speed (Yellow)

There is a constant stream of particles flowing from the Sun outwards into the solar system. Solar wind speed is the rate that these particles are moving as they pass the measurement station. Typical, ambient, solar wind speed is around 300 kilometres per second. During a strong high-speed wind stream generated by a coronal hole wind speeds can increase to between 500 and 750 km/s. Strong **CMEs** (coronal mass ejections) will also register high wind speeds and can sometimes be in excess of 1000 km/s. High solar wind speed on its own typically won't indicate that there should be aurora, but high solar wind speed can magnify the impact of the other three factors on this chart. Wind speed also impacts the lag between when charged particles and interplanetary shocks hit the satellite and when they arrive at Earth. Faster wind speeds carry those particles and charge faster. The lag determines how far in advance the wing KP model can predict KP values.

Proton Density (Orange)

Density is a measure of the number of particles that are being carried in the solar wind stream. As the density increases, the force displacing the magnetosphere increases. The combination of high density and strong solar winds together can be enough to create an aurora display. The units on the graph are parts per cubic centimetre, $p/cm3$, and anything above 30 is very dense. 30 protons per cubic centimetres may not sound like much, but remember this is space, and there are a lot of cubic centimetres.

Bt (white)

Bt is a measure of the strength of the magnetic field at the ACE satellite. Bt reacts to the interaction between the magnetic field of Earth and the magnetic field generated by the particles being carried in the solar wind. Imagine a large cloud of particles, produced by a CME on the Sun, that carry a magnetic charge passing Earth, they will exert a magnetic force on Earth as they pass. Bt measures the strength of as it passes.

Bz (red)

Bz is a measure of the direction of the magnetic field at ace. The field is three dimensional, so there are three components in the magnetic force, Bx, By, and Bz. 'Bz' is the strength of the field from the sun out through the Earth, 'By' is the strength along the parallel cutting from East to West across the equator, and 'Bz' is the parallel from the South to North Pole. Of the three, Bz has the most impact on aurora. When Bz is north (positive) the magnetic arriving from space line up with Earth and there is little interaction. When Bz is south (negative) it is opposite Earth's poles and there can be significant interaction - producing aurora. Thus, a negative Bz is almost required for aurora. All the other factors can be favourable, but if Bz is positive, pack up your camera and go home. The longer the Bz has been negative and the stronger it is negative the stronger the aurora will be. However, if the strength of the magnetic field is low, and the Bz is only registering -1 or -2 nT, aurora will be unlikely.

PHI (blue)

The phi determines whether the Interplanetary Magnetic Field (IMF) is pointed towards the Earth or away from the Earth. As phi here is determined as [0 360] within the XY plane and in the GSM coordinate system, this means that the positive X-axis is pointing from the Earth to the Sun. This means for phi = 0 the field points to the Sun and for phi=180 the field points to the Earth.

Temp (green)

The solar wind streams plasma and particles from the sun out into space. The 'temp' here literally measures the temperature of the plasma, protons, electrons, alpha particles as they come in on the solar wind. The corona, the sun's outer layer, reaches temperatures of up to 2 million degrees Fahrenheit (1.1 million Celsius). At this level, the sun's gravity/electromagnetic field can't hold on to the rapidly moving particles, and it streams away from the star.

These are the basics of our suns influence on Earth, the more charged particles we see, the more Earth changes we see.

Charged particles hit our magnetosphere, our magnetic poles pull in the particles through the magnetic attraction and that's what makes the Auroras.

Ionisation process takes place in our ionosphere, this leads to severe weather events. Like purple plasma storms, that's where a lot of land animals perish.

Plasma also has a natural plasma reaction with Earths core due to our magnetic poles being directly connected to our plasma core (which acts as a solid).

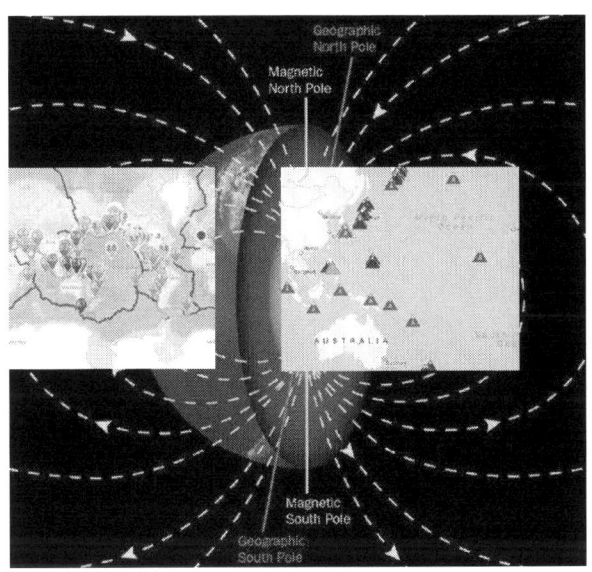

This leads to core expansion, core expansion leads to tectonic movements as the pressure builds under the plates, tectonic movements lead to Earthquakes and volcanic activity.

However, the charged particle bombardment also effects absolutely every Earth change on the planet, core expansion leads to warmer water anomalies, warmer waters leads to more extreme weather systems/depressions i.e. hurricane strength/precipitation.

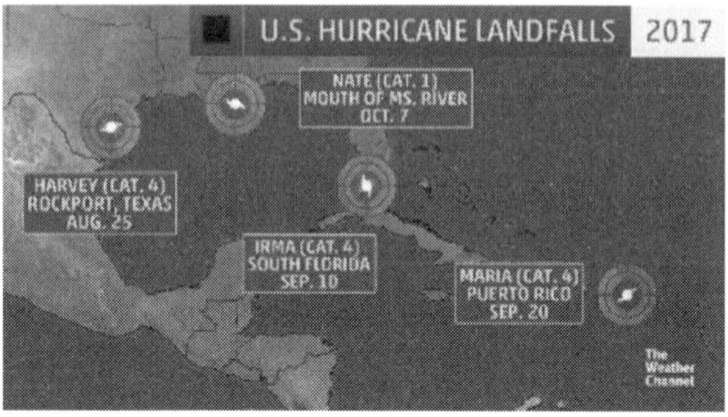
U.S. HURRICANE LANDFALLS
2017
NATE (CAT. 1)
MOUTH OF MS. RIVER
OCT. 7
HARVEY (CAT. 4)
ROCKPORT, TEXAS
AUG. 25
IRMA (CAT. 4)
SOUTH FLORIDA
SEP. 10
MARIA (CAT. 4)
PUERTO RICO
SEP. 20
The Weather Channel

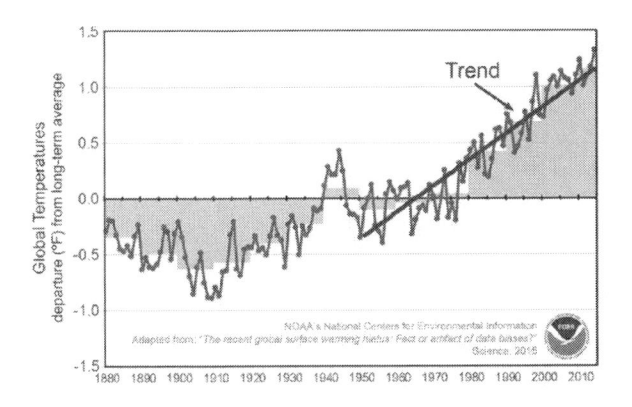

Landslides, sink holes, tidal surges, everything.

Charged particles at the poles leads to ice cap reduction, which is still losing its ice gain rapidly, winter of course, creates new ice but it's still very much reducing each year with less ice extent, as shown in previous chapters.

Charged particles causes atmospheric compressions which compresses our magnetosphere, if our magnetic field lines are disrupted then so is the wild life's navigation, that's why whales/dolphins have been washing up on shore so much because they navigate using our magnetic field. Connect the dots. Same goes for birds falling out the skies in certain areas, as already stated in the previous chapters.

The sun is being bombarded itself by a second solar wind made up of lithium/helium/iron oxide, this is coming from the solar system that's entered ours and all Earth change progression over the past 20 years is because of the interaction between this system and ours.

This is why the lithium/helium charts are also rising from satellite data, again. Connect the dots.

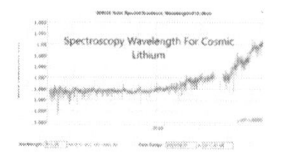

Our Earths wobble is increasing due to the magnetic strength of his system in our solar system, it's perturbing our entire system. Each time we pass it on our 365-day orbital cycle around the sun, our South Pole moves slightly as the magnetic portal connection becomes stronger, this leads to the Earths increasing wobble and pole migration and with that comes the complete intermixing of our subtropical/polar jet streams, this all adds to the extreme weather i.e. 'climate chaos'

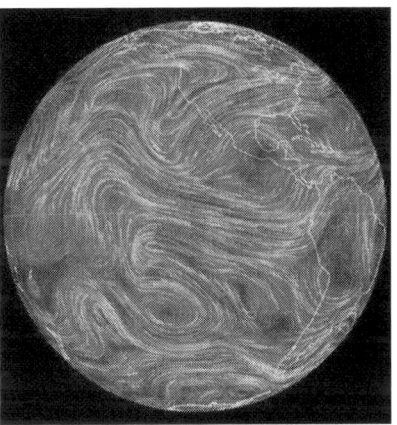

In that image, the reddish/purple parts are the Earths subtropical and pole jet streams, there should be four distinctive streams: -

Polar Jet
Subtropical Jet

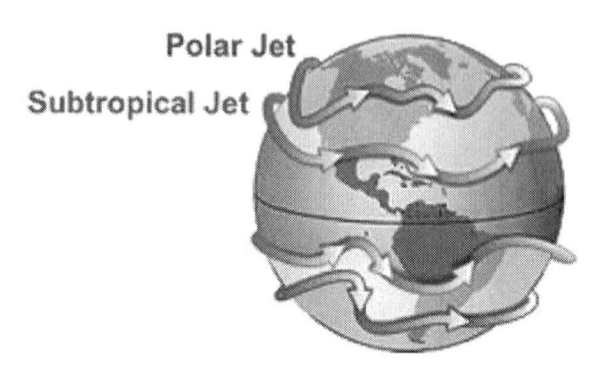

So, you can see the comparison for yourself, our subtropical and polar jet streams are intermixing all over the globe now.

Poles have been shifting for a long time now, closer the system gets, the more the polarity displacement we see.

Closer it gets, the more Earth changes we see, until it crosses Earths orbital path which is when the pole shift will occur, simple as that.

With the above understood, we can now explain more effects that the charged particles have on Earth.
It is a fact that the ozone layer in our upper atmosphere protects Earth from damaging levels of Ultra Violet radiation, right?? That's what you are lead to believe, ultra violet C being read at ground level should never

happen, ever. the ultraviolet A/B readings are reaching over 13.0 in some areas of the world. This is also very dangerous. This is happening because of the particle interaction happening to our sun due to a second solar wind, these super-heated particles get thrown at Earth causing huge atmospheric compressions, as already stated.

The shorter-wavelength, higher-energy UV radiation associated with the UVC category is very strongly absorbed by most organic materials. This is why the common 254 nm sources have become so popular for germicidal/disinfectant applications.

The strong absorption by organic molecules, including DNA, leads to severe damage to the molecule and to the organism's reproductive processes, leading to the death of the microbes.

The UVC radiation is sufficiently energetic that individual photons may produce chemical bond breakage and ionisation of some atoms and molecules.

The absorption of particular energy photons by materials, both organic and inorganic, is evident throughout the electromagnetic spectrum from microwaves through infrared and visible light, ultraviolet, x rays, and gamma rays.

The absorption at particular wavelengths may be associated with resonance-type effects in which the gaps between certain energy states in an atom or molecule are nearly matched by the energies of the incoming photons. Atomic or molecular excitation may occur as a result of the absorption, or an electron may be ejected from an atom when the incoming photon energy exceeds the binding energy of the electron in the atom.

It is common that photon absorption by particular atoms or molecules may be small at a given energy, increase with increasing energy, and then decrease again at yet higher energies, so it is not surprising that some higher-energy UV radiation may be more strongly absorbed than lower-energy UV.

In 1993, scientists at Environment Canada completed the first long-term study showing that increase in UV levels at the Earth's surface are due to thinning of the ozone layer.

Since the early 1970's chemical reactions in the environment are depleting the ozone, allowing more UV to get through. This increase in UV radiation is causing severe sun burning, eye cataracts, cancer and immune system dysfunction. Science has stepped forward to try to stop Earth's ozone destruction (chemtrails) but new evidence indicates that ozone depletion is getting worse.

Research on depletion of the ozone layer began in earnest when in 1974 two Nobel Prize winners proved that certain chemicals were destroying the ozone in our atmosphere. Since the 1970's scientists have observed a large seasonal "hole" in the ozone layer in Antarctica. Steps were taken to reduce the use of the chemicals causing this problem, and the Montreal Protocol on Substances that deplete the Ozone Layer was originally signed in 1987. Since that time, the ozone hole in the Southern Hemisphere over Antarctica has grown to as large as 25 million square miles.

In 1995, severe depletion was noted in the Northern Hemisphere as well. At that time ozone depletion of 20 to 35% was discovered in middle and high latitudes. In 1997 ozone losses over the Arctic of up to 45% were recorded and in the lower latitudes of Canada where more people live, up to 10%.

Even though steps have been taken by the world community, recent findings show that the ozone layer has not yet recovered. In fact, current ozone depletion is greater than expected.

Implications are that if this is not remedied right away, a tipping point may be reached in which a rapid, mass chemical reaction in the atmosphere could destroy immense amounts of ozone.

This would cause the sun's heat to melt two huge continents of ice in the Arctic and Antarctic. As a result, the oceans of the world would rise several feet. Then whole continents of ice could suddenly slip into the ocean causing tsunamis 100's of feet high to wash several miles inland. It could be the worst disaster the human race has ever known, well apart from the pole shift of course where we will see 400-1200ft tidal surges.

For now, we must realise that patches of thin ozone over our houses make it very dangerous to go outside at times. In northern California, in the early spring, you can be exposed to dangerously high UV levels.

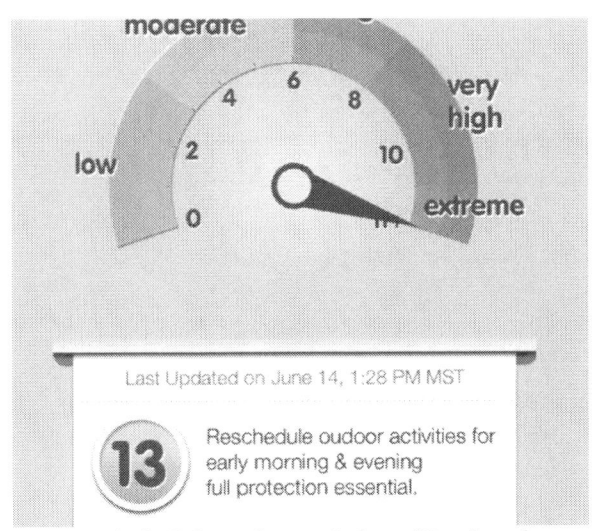

One statistic I found stated that, "During the three-day period from March 17 to 19, 2006 the total ozone cover fell below 300 DU over part of the North Atlantic region from Greenland to Scandinavia." The article warned that 300 DU is a dangerously low total ozone count. DU stands for Dobson Units which measure ozone on a scale of 0 to 500. When the DU's go as low as 220, it is considered a "hole."

I have not yet seen warnings to United States citizens about low DU readings or high UV Index readings, but I have read the DU recorded daily over areas by the National Oceanic and Atmospheric Administration (NOAA). I found several days in February and March, 2008 in which the DU's were under 300. NOAA registered readings under 300 for eleven days in February, and 12 days in March, Interestingly, the days when there were low DU readings were also the days that we saw the real thick chemtrails from jets.

The lowest point of ozone concentrations occurs in October over Antarctica and in March over the Antarctic.
People in Shasta County in Northern California took samples from ponds, HVAC filters, tops of sheds and solar panels to see what was falling out of these chemtrails.

Solar panel efficiency dropped considerably when the spraying was going on. The professional lab tests showed abnormally high and unacceptable levels of aluminium, barium and strontium.

There are no sources for these chemicals in this area except from what is falling out of the sky. Investigations of US patents indicate that these are the chemicals being sprayed to make cloud cover. After the jets spray, the DU's rise.

Citizens are not being told about these low DU readings, about the spraying nor do we ever get UV alerts like they get in Australia, well not the real readings, they massively underplay the readings all over the world.

TheOzoneHole.com has charts showing large patches of thinning ozone over the northern hemisphere. Most of Canada, Greenland, Iceland, the UK and Europe are right underneath these thinning areas. They say that, "An Arctic Ozone Hole, if similar in size to the Antarctic Ozone Hole, could expose over 700+ million people, wildlife and plants to dangerous UV ray levels. The likely hood of this happening seems inevitable based on the deterioration of ozone layer caused by the effects of global warming on the upper atmosphere."

I think it is already a dangerous situation. Why aren't we being alerted to the fact that dangerous levels of UV are penetrating the ozone layer all over the Earth?

According to NASA scientist, Jim Hansen, we are dangerously close to a 'tipping point" in which a warming climate will feed back on itself amplifying the warming effects. In May of 2007, ABC News released a report on this

NASA/Columbia study which said we only have 10 more years of "business as usual" creating emission from the burning of coal, oil and gas. The lead author of this paper, Jim Hansen is director of NASA's Goddard Institute for Space Studies in New York. According to the report, if we do not act in time, "it becomes impractical" to avoid "disastrous effects." However, this is just statements to cover up the real reason why all this is happening, the closer the planetary bodies get to the proximity of our sun, the more ozone layer depletion we see due to the particle bombardment coming in on the solar wind.

The man-made ozone that forms in the troposphere is extremely toxic and corrosive. People who inhale ozone during repeated exposure may permanently damage their lungs or suffer from respiratory infections. Ozone exposure may reduce lung function or aggravate existing respiratory conditions such as asthma, emphysema or bronchitis. Ozone may also cause chest pain, coughing, throat irritation or congestion.

The adverse health effects of ground-level ozone are particularly dangerous for people who work, exercise, or spend a lot of time outdoors during warm weather. Seniors and children are also at greater risk than the rest of the population, because people in both age groups are more likely to have reduced or not fully formed lung capacity.

Ground-level ozone also kills many seedlings and damages foliage, making trees more susceptible to diseases, pests and harsh weather.

Ultraviolet-B radiation (UV-B: - 290-315 nm) is expected to increase as the result of stratospheric ozone depletion. Within the environmental range, UV-B effects on host plants appear to be largely a function of photomorphogenic responses, while effects on fungal pathogens may include both photomorphogenesis and damage. The effects of increased UV-B on plant-pathogen interactions has been studied in only a few pathosystems, and have used a wide range of techniques, making generalisations difficult.

Increased UV-B after inoculation tends to reduce disease, perhaps due to direct damage to the pathogen, although responses vary markedly between and within pathogen species. Using Septoria tritici infection of wheat as a model system, it is suggested that even in a species that is inherently sensitive to UV-B, the effects of ozone depletion in the field are likely to be small compared with the effects of variation in UV-B due to season and varying cloud.

This year was the largest ever recorded in the Northern Hemisphere and spread over parts of northern Russia, Greenland and Norway. The magnetic north is over in Siberia now.

For the first time, the hole was comparable to one that appears regularly over the Antarctic. The ozone layer in the upper stratosphere provides a shield against UV radiation from the sun that can cause skin cancer and cataracts, without this shield, UVC is now reaching ground level, this is highly dangerous to all life, plantation, animal and human, also it will continue to melt our ice caps at an alarming rate.

The hole in the northern hemisphere coverers two million square kilometres (about twice the size of Ontario for my American friends) and allowed high levels of harmful ultraviolet radiation to hit large swaths of northern Canada, Europe and Russia this year, 29 scientists say this also. The discovery of the "unprecedented" hole comes as the Canadian government is moving to cut its ozone monitoring network; again, this is all down to the system entering our solar system, it has played havoc on every planet and is effecting our central body (sun) thus effecting Earth.

The bottom line here is they have articles out there to tell people anything they want to hear, and agencies that exist to lie about obvious and glaring truths with official approval by their governments. There are 'bottom of the barrel' paid disinformation "trolls" that live off their efforts to tarnish the truth with impressive looking charts and graphs. From the fictitious "recovering economy" to the Fukushima lies, environmental cover ups, etc. Lots of impressive looking data that adds up to total disinformation.

Primary disinformation paid trolls have said for years there is no geoengineering, no increase in droughts, no increase in floods, no increase in wildfires, etc. The increase in UV radiation facts needs to be shared and shared to as many as possible.

We all love the sun, we live going to the beach, we love BBQ's etc but we should take specific precautions when out in the sun due to these UVC readings, it's a silent killer, attacks your organs slowly, it will give you headaches, heart problems and so on. It cannot be hidden once widely known.

Attempts to 'debunk' our data on the extremely high UV levels have been short lived.

If you care about the truth, if you care about protecting the planets ability to continue sustaining life, if you care about our collective futures, do some research yourself. Look at the links. Remember that you can always find conflicting data, but what does the reality on the ground, combined with available research studies lead you to believe in regard to who has it right with the facts and who is lying their backsides off?

Supplements we should all be taking: -

Spirulina
Chlorella
Activated charcoal
Super sea kelp
Co-q10
Himalayan pink salt

The co-q10 should be taken first thing in the morning with the super sea kelp, this will regulate your heart and block radiation.

The activated charcoal I personally take in the evening so it absorbs most of the metal particulates in my body that they spray whilst I sleep.

The rest can be taken whenever through the day.

Also, I would suggest getting an orgonite pyramid for good energy surroundings, plus an orgonite pendant to prevent harmful EMF from entering your body.

Also, make sure you are mixing then drinking apple cider vinegar, lemon juice, cranberry juice in a half pint of water everyday also ...just two bottle caps full mixed in a half pint of water. This will level your alkaline levels and your body will regain its natural PH levels, this will fight cancer cells.
Below is some links to chemtrail patents and links to ozone deterioration etc. I've only added some of the patents I have because there is just too many.

Please, look them up.

http:-//www.google.com/patents/US8967029

http:-//www.google.com/patents/US1338343?printsec=abstract&dq=1338343&ei=Xm9LUJCRCImQ9QS1-4GADg#v=onepage&q=1338343&f=false

http:-//www.google.com/patents/US1619183?printsec=abstract&dq=1619183&ei=TW9LUP-OGIGC8QTAl4G4BQ#v=onepage&q=1619183&f=false

http:-//www.google.com/patents/US1631753?printsec=abstract&dq=1631753&ei=PW9LUIKROIrI9QSx3YDQCg#v=onepage&q=1631753&f=false

http:-//www.google.com/patents/US1665267?printsec=abstract&dq=1665267&ei=L29LULjPEIWo8gS9m4GIAg#v=onepage&q=1665267&f=false

http:-//www.google.com/patents/US1892132?printsec=abstract&dq=1892132&ei=H29LUMLuEY

W29QSVmoCICA#v=onepage&q=1892132&f=false

http:-//www.google.com/patents/US1928963?printsec=abstract&dq=1928963&ei=CW9LUOH8E4Wa9gS_sYHoCQ#v=onepage&q=1928963&f=false

http:-//www.google.com/patents/US1957075?printsec=abstract&dq=1957075&ei=-m5LUO6pOImu8ASTl4GYBg#v=onepage&q=1957075&f=false

http:-//www.google.com/patents/US2097581?printsec=abstract&dq=2097581&ei=6W5LUILkOIKa9gSs_oBo#v=onepage&q=2097581&f=false

http:-//www.google.com/patents/US2409201?printsec=abstract&dq=2409201&ei=2G5LUNzLKojo8gSjtoHYDg#v=onepage&q=2409201&f=false

http:-//www.google.com/patents/US2476171?printsec=abstract&dq=2476171&ei=yG5LUNzjF4Gg9QTkvYGoBA#v=onepage&q=2476171&f=false

http:-//www.google.com/patents/US2480967?printsec=abstract&dq=2480967&ei=t25LUKj4OYiu9ASNwoDoAg#v=onepage&q=2480967&f=false

http:-//www.google.com/patents/US2550324?printsec=abstract&dq=2550324&ei=pm5LUNKKEJHi9gTxjoDoBg#v=onepage&q=2550324&f=false

http:-//www.google.com/patents/US2582678?printsec=abstract&dq=2582678&ei=MG5LUIOOGYrW9QSQ8oHIAQ#v=onepage&q=2582678&f=false

http:-//www.google.com/patents/US2591988?printsec=abstract&dq=2591988&ei=Bm5LULXxEYb48gSOxYHABQ#v=onepage&q=2591988&f=false

http:-//www.google.com/patents/US2614083?printsec=abstract&dq=2614083&ei=821LUMiJOYa09QSqgIG4Cg#v=onepage&q=2614083&f=false

http://www.google.com/patents/US2633455?printsec=abstract&dq=2633455&ei=4m1LUILpIoLo9AS_loBA#v=onepage&q=2633455&f=false

http://www.google.com/patents/US2721495?printsec=abstract&dq=2721495&ei=vm1LUK3HJIaA9QSsu4CgDA#v=onepage&q=2721495&f=false

http://www.google.com/patents/US2730402?printsec=abstract&dq=2730402&ei=rG1LUJ_yOI_m8QSl3IHICQ#v=onepage&q=2730402&f=false

http://www.google.com/patents/US2801322?printsec=abstract&dq=2801322&ei=lW1LUOL0Co-89gSLkYGgCw#v=onepage&q=2801322&f=false

http://www.google.com/patents/US2881335?printsec=abstract&dq=2881335&ei=g21LUMLlOpCE8ATetoHYBQ#v=onepage&q=2881335&f=false

http://www.google.com/patents/US2908442?printsec=abstract&dq=2908442&ei=bG1LUNibEYu-9QT20oCQCw#v=onepage&q=2908442&f=false

http://www.google.com/patents/US2986360?printsec=abstract&dq=2986360&ei=Wm1LUPSTLIO8wSfooGgBQ#v=onepage&q=2986360&f=false

http://www.google.com/patents/US2963975?printsec=abstract&dq=2963975&ei=R21LULSTKYTY8gTL6YDgCA#v=onepage&q=2963975&f=false

http://www.google.com/patents/US3126155?printsec=abstract&dq=3126155&ei=MW1LUKOYKIbM9gS3kIGIBw#v=onepage&q=3126155&f=false

http://www.google.com/patents/US3127107?printsec=abstract&dq=3127107&ei=Hm1LUN69PIf28wSozYDoCQ#v=onepage&q=3127107&f=false

http://www.google.com/patents/US3131131?printsec=abstract&dq=3131131&ei=_mxLUKf0DYym8ASA4YH4Bw#v=onepage&q=3131131&f=false

http://www.google.com/patents/US3174150?printsec=abstract&dq=3174150&ei=6WxLULHqBYKc9gTgqYD4BA#v=onepage&q=3174150&f=false

http://www.google.com/patents/US3234357?printsec=abstract&dq=3234357&ei=0WxLUIarG5GO9AS404HACg#v=onepage&q=3234357&f=false

http://www.google.com/patents/US3274035?printsec=abstract&dq=3274035&ei=v2xLUOepCpSQ8wSo_YC4Bg#v=onepage&q=3274035&f=false

http://www.google.com/patents/US3300721?printsec=abstract&dq=3300721&ei=rGxLUNf9BITi8gSRzIHYDQ#v=onepage&q=3300721&f=false

http://www.google.com/patents/US3313487?printsec=abstract&dq=3313487&ei=mGxLUNyjJ4iK9QT334GoBg#v=onepage&q=3313487&f=false

http://www.google.com/patents/US3338476?printsec=abstract&dq=3338476&ei=hGxLUNnOM4is8ATY74DwDQ#v=onepage&q=3338476&f=false

http://www.google.com/patents/US3410489?printsec=abstract&dq=3410489&ei=cWxLUOvME46a9QTLy4GoAw#v=onepage&q=3410489&f=false

http://www.google.com/patents/US3429507?printsec=abstract&dq=3429507&ei=X2xLUL3BJ4a09gSA7gE#v=onepage&q=3429507&f=false

http://www.google.com/patents/US3432208?printsec=abstract&dq=3432208&ei=TWxLULLWBoaS9gSInYDgCw#v=onepage&q=3432208&f=false

http://www.google.com/patents/US3445844?printse

c=abstract&dq=3445844&ei=J2xLUJSwKIe29QSf9IGICQ#v=onepage&q=3445844&f=false

http:-//www.google.com/patents/US3456880?printsec=abstract&dq=3456880&ei=D2xLUNOgJYK29gS-4oDwDg#v=onepage&q=3456880&f=false

http:-//www.google.com/patents/US3518670?printsec=abstract&dq=3518670&ei=SWtLUKuuCIiE8ASkhIGYDw#v=onepage&q=3518670&f=false

http:-//www.google.com/patents/US3534906?printsec=abstract&dq=3534906&ei=NmtLUK76BoK29gS-4oDwDg#v=onepage&q=3534906&f=false

http:-//www.google.com/patents/US3564253?printsec=abstract&dq=3564253&ei=B2tLUNjPC4Hs8gSH_IHgBQ#v=onepage&q=3564253&f=false

http:-//www.google.com/patents/US3587966?printsec=abstract&dq=3587966&ei=6GpLUL_dL4r4

9QTTnICwBA#v=onepage&q=3587966&f=false

http://www.google.com/patents/US3601312?printsec=abstract&dq=3601312&ei=P2pLUOLLHZTS8wS4moCoAg#v=onepage&q=3601312&f=false

http://www.google.com/patents/US3608810?printsec=abstract&dq=3608810&ei=JmpLUJjBLpHo8wSv9IGwBA#v=onepage&q=3608810&f=false

http://www.google.com/patents/US3608820?printsec=abstract&dq=3608820&ei=DWpLUMuWEoOC9gTz-IDQCQ#v=onepage&q=3608820&f=false

http://www.google.com/patents/US3613992?printsec=abstract&dq=3613992&ei=EWlLUJ60OIfk9ASnj4DwBw#v=onepage&q=3613992&f=false

https://www2.ucar.edu/atmosnews/news/942/stratospheric-injections-counter-global-warming-could-damage-ozone-layer

http:-//www.gma.org/surfing/human/ozonephyto.html

https:-//www.scientificamerican.com/article/phytoplankton-population/

https:-//www.for.gov.bc.ca/hfd/pubs/docs/lmh/Lmh49.pdf

So, all geological changes of Earth will continue to increase as the system gets closer: -

Charged particle stream
Ionospheric heating
Sea temperature anomalies
Core expansion
Ice cap reduction
Plasma storms
Hurricanes
Tornados
Volcanic eruptions
Sink holes
Landslides
Earthquakes
Tidal surges
Tidal retreats

The list goes on.

Earth's rotation will begin to slow gradually as the systems magnetic influence becomes too strong for Earth's magnetic field which will also change the core dynamics of Earth, this is another reason the tectonic shifting becomes increasingly dramatic and our magnetosphere begins to weaken even more than it already is.

Even though I have spoken of this for many years, I'm not the only person that is talking about this either, the mainstream scientists of the world are now speaking of the pole shift and the slowing rotation of Earth.

CHAPTER 6

NIBIRU/NEMESIS CONDITIONING

In this chapter; I've put together some images from the videos that contain the best of subliminal messaging about the solar system that's entered ours.

This is how the elite work, it's a universal law that they have to show you what's coming and they have been doing it for many years.

From kid's television shows, TV commercials, music videos, films, magazines, billboards, logos, brands and so on. To the untrained eye this would go unnoticed but it would be logged in your subconscious unwillingly, it's a form of brainwashing which they utilise very well.

I can guarantee you this- the 2000/2012 end of the world predictions are/were designed by the elite to create mass hysteria so that the dates come and go without anything happening which makes you naturally adopt this "well they said it would happen back then and it didn't, what a load of crap" kind of attitude which plays straight into the elite's hands, they actually depend on your ignorance.

It's about connecting all the dots, if you follow my posts on Facebook I'm pretty sure you'll agree that there is far too much evidence to ignore so please don't let the modern-day attitude of 'ignorance' stop you from using your critical thinking brain and think outside the box.

It's all coming, it's here, it's soon. Whether it's this year or 5 years- it's still soon.

Pole shift is imminent.

The first one I want to touch on is a music video from the '2cellos' called 'the show must go on', they are a classical music duo, very well known throughout the classical music industry which is usually of a wealthy backing smothered in Masonic ties. The duo are just the puppets in front of the cameras, the real people behind these video masterpieces are the producers who are heavily involved in the occult and love to give subliminal messages through music, as you will see in the next set of images that I have pulled from the video: -

As you can see, the video gets straight into the subliminal messages where it shows two planetary bodies beginning to interact with Earth.

Next, we see a huge planetary body in the background with electronic billboards showing 'evacuation' news statements.

Here we see the road signs stating 'no admittance' which is one of the main things I talk about when martial law is in force.

Then we see your everyday people with survival bags looking for places to hide.

As the scenes go on, we see more planetary bodies which is causing worldwide panic and tidal surges.

So, as you can see, the music video is portraying a planetary body causing a pole shift, with roads blocked and people trying to survive.

As always- they have to show you what's coming. To see this music video in full please copy this link-
https://youtu.be/L051v3NC0F4

The next set of images are from the film 'GEOSTORM' which I have seen, if you haven't watched it then please do as you can get a first-hand view of the subliminal messages: -

Tidal surges.

From the trailer of the movie- reference to 'HAARP'.

Tornados will be very sporadic in the future as we get closer to the pole shift, as well as hurricanes.

Burst gas pipes/magma intrusions. This is already happening as we speak but will continue to intensify as time goes on, the volcanic increase now seems bad with the recent Guatemala and Hawaii eruptions (2018) but this will also increase in intensification. Water main bursts/train derailments/gas main bursts/sink holes= ground movement.

This scene shows an instant freeze phase which will happen in certain areas due to there being an extreme amount of force being created from the atmospheric compressions and the hurricanes, these events will be in isolated areas, not worldwide.

To see the full trailer, please copy this link- https:-//youtu.be/Qz8cjvKJLuw

The next set are taken from the music video by 'the Weeknd' called 'I Feel It Coming': -

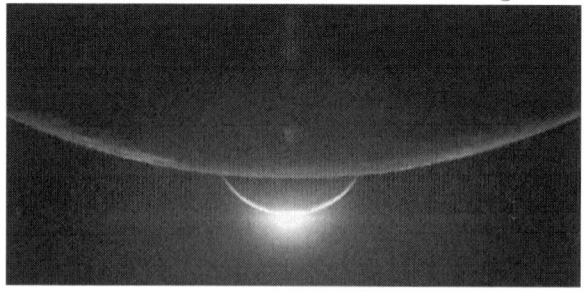

As you can clearly see, they get straight into it.

The 'second sun' showing an appearance.

This scene shows the 'nemesis' star system which is shown in previous chapters, very similar formation also.

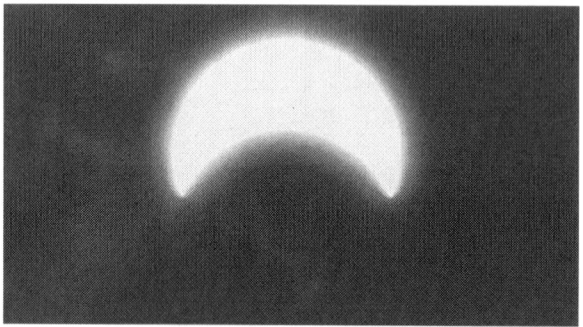

As the video goes on, they depict the 'perihelion' stage of the crossing where the sun will be dark for 3 days as the planetary bodies cross Earths orbital path creating an eclipse between the sun and Earth.

perihelion stage, the skies begin to turn a plasmatic red colour due to the interplanetary electromagnetic forces interacting.

After that, desolation.

To see the full music video please copy this link- https:-//youtu.be/qFLhGq0060w

The next set of still shots is from the movie trailer 'The day after tomorrow' which is one of the best depictions of a pole shift.

The birds/animals will always be the first to act strange due to them using our magnetic field

as navigation, when our magnetosphere is compressed, the animals will be confused.

Always listen/watch nature- it never lies.

Her we see the masses trying to find safety before it's too late. This is reality, the masses will get little warning of these coming events so is better to be ready before the public statement is announced. Keep watching my posts as well as others, we will always bring you truth.

High tidal surges- one of the biggest events of the pole shift. All coastal areas will see 400-1200ft high tidal surges and some places will see 1800ft high surges due to tidal bore as the waters meet narrower land mass i.e. rivers/sea inlets/valleys etc.

To watch the full trailer, please copy this link- https:-//youtu.be/Ku_IseK3xTc

The next set are from the film 'Deep impact' which also has lots of in your face subliminal messaging: -

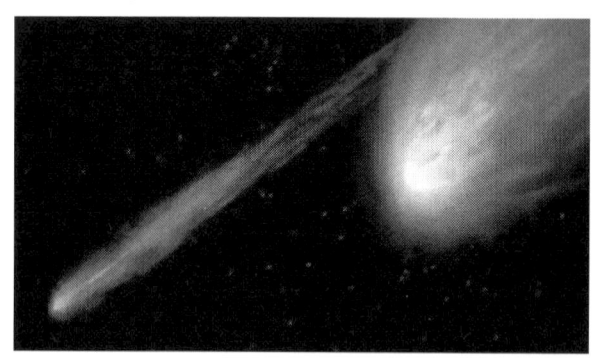

Here we see the representation of nemesis and nibiru, although they portray these planetary objects to be asteroids in the film, I can assure you that they know exactly what they represent.

Here we see the 'selected' being taken to the DUMB cities (deep underground military bases, these bases exist now and are readily prepped for the coming events.

Here we see more road blockages through the panic of the cataclysm.

Then the great tidal surges.

To see the full trailer, please copy this link-
https:-//youtu.be/NTkfk4dCnu8

There are many other films/adverts/cartoons/logos that all leave subliminal messages that would go unnoticed but I will add some images so you can get a perspective of just how 'in your face' it is: -

Billboard advert, notice the red planet flying past Earth.

The WEIRDEST VISITOR The Earth Has Ever Seen!
Sherrill Corwin
THE MAN FROM PLANET X
Starring
ROBERT CLARKE
MARGARET FIELD
RAYMOND BOND
Directed by EDGAR G. ULMER
Written and Produced by AUBREY WISBERG and JACK POLLEXFEN
UNITED ARTISTS

U.S. AIR FORCE

BENTLEY

IllinoisTimes

32 HOLIDAY | *Polar Express* 3 OPINION | Election news 26 FOOD | Edible holiday gifts

PERISHING PLANET

Call to action on climate change

16 ENVIRONMENT | Aheali Bland

Films like '2012' are great depictions of times leading up to the pole shift/during shift/post shift as well as films like- San Andreas/Earthquake/Dante's Peak/day after tomorrow/deep impact/Armageddon/hunger games/divergent/maze runner/total recall. All dystopian films portray post shift, all geological catastrophe films portray the before/during shift.

Here some more links to music videos/film trailers that show all kinds of symbolism/subliminal messaging: -
https:-//youtu.be/Ku_IseK3xTc

https:-//youtu.be/NQKz5eHGx1k

https:-//youtu.be/kszLwBaC4Sw

https:-//youtu.be/NTkfk4dCnu8

https:-//youtu.be/cjvmRUVnfpk

https:-//youtu.be/rvI66Xaj9-o

https:-//youtu.be/oznEkwtasBk

https:-//youtu.be/23VflsU3kZE

https:-//youtu.be/OiPBlc9wBGI

FINAL CHAPTER

What to expect, Safe locations- how to survive.

This will be the most important chapter for those who have the will and determination to survive the coming events, it is always better to be prepared for any event, whether it be war/water shortage/hurricanes/volcanic activity etc, being prepared is half the battle.

Ok... tell tail signs of the pole shift.

6+ Earthquakes in the Atlantic ridge.

If Japan splits and one part goes under.

If Australia's west coast subsides.

If nuclear war breaks out.

If the internet shuts down.

If the power in general shuts down.

If the sun rises in the west.

If 'aliens' are announced to have been found publicly.

The alien announcement will be to implement the fake alien invasion to create worldwide martial law.

If any of the above starts to happen, two weeks to get the hell out of the cities/towns and get to safe locations. Things might take a couple of months to take effect but you need to stay in the safe location from that two-week warning.

The last place you want to be is in a city or town, they will be rife with violence/panic, there are horrible people in the world now so you can imagine what it will be like when the streets are lawless with all people trying to fight for their family's survival.

Pole shift- what to expect.

This is 14 years' worth of deep study so it makes no difference to me whether you want to believe it or not, I know the truth and have tried to connect all the dots so the knowledge can be shared with as many people as possible.

Pole shift means the oceans will slosh causing worldwide costal 500ft plus tidal surges with it reaching 1200-1500ft above sea level due to tidal bore.

They have been building sea defence systems since I was a child worldwide because they knew these days was coming.

Build-up/close to and in the hour of the shift- The wind will exceed 200mph-600mph, there will be fast moving cyclones/hurricanes ...there will be sudden plasma storms/ice storms.... you see the films day after tomorrow or 2012? If you have then that's the best depiction of a pole shift.

Not only that, we will be getting meteorites raining down on Earth as we will be directly in the debris field of the system.

Crustal displacement- this means huge geological changes, some land will rise up, some land will go under water....so I'd suggest being in a craton plate if your near one.

So, in other words, in the hour of the pole shift you need to be underground, in a cave at least away from the coastlines and as high as possible.

They will use war as a disguise for this, hence the news saying 'president Putin of Russia has been secretly planting nuclear bombs on the US coasts that will cause a huge tsunami', Those sorts of headlines are just a cover, there are bombs, all the effects of the bombs causing a tsunami will be so that when it passes they can legitimately go to war even more to succeed their 'new world order'.

So, before war- martial law, look out for big false flags, this is merely a way of gaining more control. martial law will keep you exactly where they want you to be...and don't be fooled, they have an elite army that's paid for out of the 'black op' funds, you know, the billions of pounds/dollars that go missing every year without a trace? so don't think for one second, they care if they lose the standard military, to them they are expendable and are there to keep everything going to plan. So, if you hear anything about martial on the news, you know it's close...they have already shipped hundreds of thousands of 'martial law' signs around the world which is also easily researched, I wonder why?

FEMA/UN camps already pre-built all over the world, some are tactically hidden and disguised as normal buildings ready and waiting to house the civilians that are left...don't take my word for it, go do some digging and I'm sure you'll easily find out just how well prepared the elite are for these coming events.

Yep, hard to believe, hard to swallow and hard to comprehend but remember that this plan has been in the making for a very long time.

As previously stated the elite have underground D.U.M.B cities built in preparation for all this.

This happens every 3600 + years as it makes its way back on its elliptical orbit.

No this isn't a normal cycle, well it depends what you class as normal because I suppose it's natural, the last pole shift is why there are cities under water and why big boats were found in mountains, the plasma discharges in the atmosphere is what the ancient use to draw on walls, the dragon in Chinese prophecy is the plasma reactions that go from planet to planet as they draw close, the tribulation in the bible is the crossing, blue &a red kachina in the Hopi prophecies are nemesis and nibiru, the destroyer is what they called it in Hebrew, the winged sun symbol is what they used in ancient Egypt due to its looking like it has wings from the red iron oxide particles spewing off it as it makes its orbit around nemesis, the ancient Sumerians called it the red dragon/nibiru, ancient Indians called it the winged serpent...every religion has the same exact story just interpreted in different ways, they had the same paintings/carvings all over the world without being able to contact each other and all predate to over 3500+ years ago...

It's about connecting the dots, the 'signs In the heavens' that's talked about in revelations is the plasma reactions and fireballs that we are seeing now, the 'sound of trumpets' in the bible, which is being heard in some parts of the worlds is crustal displacement that resonates off of the oceans and echoes through the atmosphere along with the atmosphere being compressed with gamma rays that disrupt our magnetic field lines and cause the same 'trumpet' sound, the huge increase in Earthquakes/volcanoes is what's referred to in the bible as 'birth pains' and the magma chambers being pressurised causes gas releases which create a screeching sound; also being heard more in these days.

All the fish are dying by the thousands, birds are dying through magnetic field line disruptions, land animals are being killed in the thousands before plasma storms-

I've studied the bible, the Sumerian tablets, the Incas, Mayans, Hopi and pretty much all over books of knowledge like the Kolbrin bible, lost book of enki, book of Enoch and it all categorically points to the crossing and all the effects leading up to it.

Worst places and best places to be during/near the pole shift -

Remember, some land will rise, some land will subside. Imagine being in the middle of the Atlantic when the Atlantic ridge separates? Boats will not be able to deal with that kind of movement.

Remember, new faults will occur along the sea beds and under water volcanoes will be extremely violent.

Worst places-

Middle of the sea in any kind of boat.

By coastal areas.

Near fault lines.

Near volcanoes.

Near rivers.

Near dams.

Near nuclear power plants.

Near cities.

Near towns.

*
*

Best places-

100 miles from any nuclear power plant.

As far in land as possible.

Nowhere near volcanoes, even dormant ones.

At least 1200ft above sea level.

In a cave on solid foundations.

In an underground structure on solid foundations.

That's the basics for the shift.

Ps. Don't follow **FEMA**, don't follow **UN** and don't follow the instructions that they give on the mainstream media news when these days come.

Get to secluded locations, start anew.

This will help those that are struggling with what to have in your survival kits.

As there is loads of newcomers, this is highly important-

SURVIVAL BAG and alternative routes: -

These are the must haves, the things that you will need bring with you, not just for you but for the whole group also.

We will be farming our own foods, purifying our own water and creating our own energy so these things are a must have for everyone to have that want to survive and thrive together as a whole to build a better community.

Seeds- fruit, herb and vegetable seeds will play a huge role in keeping our community fed and a thriving farmland is a thriving community. MUST be ORGANIC. Use the seeds that grow within to regrow your vegetation.

Water- get some pallets of bottled water to the safe locations for the first period of the transition but hopefully, there will be water sources there that you can distil daily for our communities uses, however, make sure you have a couple of bottles of water in your bag, also it's a must to have water purification tablets, they are very cheap to buy and don't take up any room at all so please invest in them if you haven't already. Also, take as much water in your vehicles as possible when the time comes.

Food- you will all need to ideally bring 3 months' worth of food rations for each person you bring to the safe location, it sounds a lot but be sensible with the types of food you pack. Ideally you want dried vegetables/berries/fruit/cereal bars/energy bars/glucose tablets/multivitamins/rice that kind of stuff will be much easier to keep and is easy to buy in bulk. Also, protein powder contains an abundance of nutrition and again is easy to stock up. This is all needed for when we are waiting for our food to grow etc and we will also be hunting/fishing daily.

Alternative power- we will be creating our own power but the initial first couple of weeks will be where we are building these systems so please try to bring batteries, preferably rechargeable ones. Wind up torch/lanterns/radios is good to have especially the ones with USB build in. Solar panel energy will be idea for when the sun is out and there are a variety of portable panel systems that are available. You can also create power from plants which is something worth researching. Water can be converted into energy with a rotational contraption which is also worth researching.

Shelter- now this is totally your choice on what sort of shelter you want to be in for the first part of the transition, we would all love a swanky caravan ideally but it just won't be the case. I personally think the pop-up tents are essential for everyone's list as they self-erect themselves, ideal for when we are on foot and the roads are blocked. Of course, if we can access the safe location by vehicle then you could pack any tent but be prepared for all situations. This is for pre-shift and post shift, you'll need to be in an underground, strong structure for the shift transition.

HAM radio handset- this is a **MUST** have for everyone in the group, probably one of the most essential parts of your survival equipment, this will be your form of contact with the whole group as you near the safe locations so that you can find your fellow people. Ideally you want one handset per person you bring to the safe locations but one handset per each group will still be better than none. You should set up your own call sign when you have a handset and have a set channel for your community to use.

Basic Survival equipment- we have done a few videos for people to get a better idea of what we personally have in our bags but it's your own preference really. Essentially you need to have- fire lighting equipment, compass, maps, survival knife, mini fishing kit, waterproof clothing, basic food rations, water purification tablets (note- there are many different types, you should get the ones that purify 1 litre to each tablet and get the ones that purify 25-30 litres per tablet), survival books, emergency tent, torch, sleeping bag, body wash, camping saucepans, water storage and your **HAM** radio handset. Again, if we can get there by car before SHTF then take as much stuff as you can, above is just basic MUST HAVES.

Alternative routes- it is up to every individual to get to know every other route possible to get to the safe location, it's essential to know these routes guys I can't stress this enough because we all know the roads will be blocked at some stage and when martial law is announced the military will be swiftly ordered to close roads so familiarise yourself with walking/cycling/cross country/driving routes and also if you don't know how to read a compass/map then please take 5 minute to watch a video on how to because it's very simple an easy to learn.

Hope this helps some that are still wondering what to bring/pack.

This transition will be hard for everyone but we WILL survive and we will beat the elite to gain peace on Earth, the elite will try to survive and try to carry on this slavery system they have put us in to chase imaginary paper that's worthless...but they will fail eventually.

The pole shift is a great opportunity to meet fellow survivalists that are preparing for the same events, you will have an instant bond with these people for they are on the same wavelength as you.

This will give you the foundations to start a thriving community with people that have the best intentions for humans and Mother Nature, you won't need a 'leader' or a 'higher power' to lead your community, all you need is people with knowledge to guide others, all members will learn something new from each member, make group decisions whilst finding common ground.

The last thing a survival group needs is arrogance/ego/pride/alphas. That's what went wrong with the world in the first place because that leads to 'governments'.

Your community will be your new family; a bunch of people all brought together through truth and the will to survive; learn to trust and care for your new family; fight for them against the other groups that survive who won't come in peace. Violence is the very last resort but there will be groups out there that will just want to take all your stock, if trading doesn't work and they become forceful then you will have to protect your own whilst knowing you are doing it for the good of the community.

We have a real chance to get Earth back to he way it should be after the pole shift, a chance to be unshackled from the daily struggle of trying to earn your daily wages from a system they have imprisoned us in, a chance to farm your own foods, source your own water, build your own houses from the natural materials Earth has provided us with in abundance...be at one with nature once more just like the ancient civilisations were.

No one is truly safe in a pole shift event....

But I will never give up, never stop fighting and I'll die for our community when the time comes.

We're stronger together.

Stay vigilant, stay positive and most of all LOVE.

Trusted sources, people to follow

You can find all these people on my Facebook page when searching in the 'friends' bar: -

Steve from the YouTube channel: - sky watch media news, independent and very in-depth videos that cover all aspects of the incoming planetary system. He covers a lot of geological events and solar anomalies that all tie in to the coming events, he puts in the hours freely for the public and has always stuck to scientific based data.

Laura Wells who spends a lot of time researching and spreading knowledge and has a sharp eye for solar/geological/political changes of Earth, Laura is also an administrator of my Facebook group which now has over 25,000 people in and I must say a special thank you to her for being my eyes and ears when I'm not available.

Justin Moats, very knowledgeable man, especially when it comes to Astro/particle physics and has a great understanding of how the interplanetary electromagnetic energy works, also a special thank you for all the times I've tagged your name in a post that needs answering when I've been busy.

Lee Inskip, he covers the Sirius star system in-depth from all angles and tirelessly posts lots of good information that coincides with the Egyptian/annunaki eras, very passionate about his work and I very much respect that.

Serenity Elmo, a true friend, a fellow prepper and the founder of our survival community. He has lots of knowledge on the global anomalies/solar anomalies that we are seeing. He has a wide field of knowledge on the Hopi prophecies and always shares knowledge when he can. He sees the exact same things I see and knows what's coming.

MRMBB333 on YouTube is an independent researcher who covers lots of geological/Earth changes and gives pre-warnings when hurricanes/storms are going to hit certain areas.

Kelley Orion, a very inspirational woman who always has a positive outlook on life, when it comes to spirituality. Kelley is at one with the universe and is a perfect example of how your consciousness should be in these troubled times. An honour to be amongst your presence.

I could add lots of people to that list but some wish not to be named which I totally understand...but you know who you are.

The people I want to thank the most is all the beautiful followers/friends/group members/survival members- **THANK YOU.**

You are my inspiration and the reason why I do what I do...I'm for the people, I'm one of the people and I'll always try to be the good. In a very bad society.

Oh.. and one more thank you- UNIVERSE/LOVE.

Our Facebook group - https:-//m.facebook.com/groups/208360166188617

My page- https:-//www.facebook.com/hiddenknowledge.unravellingthepoleshift/

My other page- https:-//www.facebook.com/knowtruth101/

Printed in Great Britain
by Amazon